CONTENTS

GUESS WHAT? YOU'RE A FOREIGNER

By Daniel C. Messina

I hope you'll enjoy reading this book!

Daniel Messina

This world is not my home. I'm just passing through." Daniel Messina takes this well known Christian saying and shows us the beauty and challenges "Redeemed-foreigners", who live well for Jesus today, encounter on their way to a new and better Eden reserved for them in the New Heavens and New Earth. There will be much profit in setting aside some time to work through this well written book .

Daniel L. Akin, PhD
President – Southeastern Baptist Theological Seminary

"Daniel Messina is one of the sharpest young pastors in America. In this fine book, he makes the argument that, because of the Fall, each of us is a "foreigner" in a broken world. When Christ returns to set the world to rights, those who have trusted him will find themselves full citizens of Christ's kingdom. And, as the author reveals so effectively, this biblical truth has profound implications for the family, the church, and for society and culture at large. "

Bruce Riley Ashford, PhD
Senior Fellow in Public Theology at the Kirby Laing Centre (Cambridge, U.K.) and author of Letters to an American Christian (B&H) and The Gospel of our King (Baker).

I highly recommend the book "GUESS WHAT? YOU'RE A FOREIGNER" by Daniel C. Messina. I have known Daniel since his days in college and trust his judgement and his writing ability. The author compares his experience as a foreigner in America to that of a Christian being a foreigner in this world because home is in heaven. Daniel is clear in stating "The purpose of this book is to show that the Bible reveals this world is not our home: instead, we were created to dwell in God's presence and eternal kingdom forever." The first part of the book is a Biblical basis for us as Christ-followers. The second relates to the practical aspects of life for what Daniel calls "the redeemed-foreigners" concerning family, society and church. This is a handbook that I find to be a great reminder that "we are not of this world" and is helpful to keep life in perspective. The book is an easy read for Christians of all ages and helps us as we seek to understand the Kingdom of God and our role in it.

Dr. Guy Key Missionary with the International Mission Board of the SBC in Brazil since 1984 Church Planting and Mission Mobilization Strategist

I wish I could say I always live as if this world is not my home. It's easy to fall into the trap of building my own kingdom, thus living for this present world more than the one to come. For that reason, this book is both informative and convicting to me. Written by a "foreigner" who experienced challenges of living in a foreign land when he came to America, this book walks through the biblical storyline, points out foreigners God has used, and challenges us to live as "redeemed-foreigners." It is the story of God's working to redeem foreigners and make them "eternal heavenly citizens." I have been challenged again to review my attachment to the world and live as Jesus taught us to live.

Chuck Lawless, PhD
Professor of Evangelism and Missions Dean of Doctoral Studies at Southeastern Baptist

DANIEL C. MESSINA

Theological Seminary

"Guess What? You're a Foreigner," is a timely book given the recent social and political debates about immigration and racism. Such issues are certainly impacting the church and Messina's argument for "redeemed foreigners" offers an alternative picture of the heart of the Gospel using pervasive biblical concepts such as "aliens", "exile", and "citizenship." His biblical-theological analysis and contemporary application of those themes is even more compelling given that he writes from the perspective of a "foreigner."

Jake Pratt, PhD Assistant
Professor of New Testament and Hermeneutics
Director of PhD Studies at Southeastern Baptist Theological Seminary

"This world is not my home, I'm just a passin' through." The words of this old spiritual describes in a phrase a much deeper truth. We are sojourners, aliens; we are not of this world. Daniel Messina unpacks this reality in great detail in this encouraging and informative book. Drawing from his own rich experience from coming to America from his homeland of Brazil, Daniel tells the story in Scripture of redemption, foreigners being redeemed, and hope of a homeland beyond this life. As you walk through this broken world be encouraged: God is making all things new."

Alvin Reid, PhD
Author of Restoring Gratitude: Finding Beauty in Brokenness and Life Is a Mission Trip: Take It!

PREFACE

Guess what? You're a foreigner! And so am I. Have you ever felt like you were created for something more? That perhaps there is more to life? That your life's purpose, meaning, and direction are not rooted in anything this world can offer? I would venture to say you, like me, feel like there is an "otherworldly" significance to life

If you have felt there is more to life, you are right! You and I are foreigners. This world is not our permanent home.

At the most basic level we all seek meaning. We want our life to matter. You want your life to count for something, and so do I. You want to feel like you belong, especially living in a world that often marginalizes us and makes us look trivial and unimportant. Significance is something all human beings desire. Yet it often seems just beyond our grasp.

Some of us wish we could exchange our parents, while some of us wish we had parents. Some of us wish we were born into a wealthy family, while some wish for a simple life. We wish we were able to pick our societal status from birth or our appearance. And these conundrums mark just a few of the struggles related to the meaning of our lives and our existence.

"What if" questions may at one point lurk into our minds. Some of the more significant "what if" questions are: What if I was not created for this world? What if I was created for something beyond this world? What if I am just passing through this world as something much more significant awaits me in the future? What if my life's purpose transcends anything this world can or will ever be able to offer? What if I am simply a foreigner on earth? C. S. Lewis puts it this way, "If I find in myself a desire which no experience in this world can satisfy, the most probable explanation is that I was made for another world."[1]

I was born and raised in the country of Brazil. In 2002, I received the news I had been chosen to be the recipient of an "International Scholarship" from Ouachita Baptist University (OBU), in Arkadelphia, Arkansas. The full sum of this scholarship was $48.000! Coming to the United States and leaving my family at a young age was not necessarily in my plans. It seemed like this opportunity dropped out of heaven onto my lap. In Brazil, most young men and women only leave home when they get married. Most leave their parents' home when they are in their mid to late twenties. I broke the cultural norm, leaving home at age 18.

I was not prepared for what was going to happen next. I grew up in a loving family environment. I had lived in the same house, city, and attended only one church my entire life. Church was an important part of my upbringing. Did I also mention I only spoke one language at that time? It was not English! Coming to America was a challenge like none I had ever experienced.

Upon arriving in America, I was labeled a "foreigner" or an "alien" by the US government. This label made me feel inferior. I was given an alien number. An "alien" number?! ... I thought aliens were creatures from other planets! Me? An alien? At first, I was offended. The label "immigrant/foreigner/alien" made me feel like an outcast. It made me feel like I had lost my significance. It was only later that I understood we are all strangers in a foreign land. Yes, all of us. Which brings me to the title of the book: *Guess What?! ...You're a Foreigner!*

While living in a foreign land, my cultural values, religious values, and family values were profoundly challenged. For the first time in my life, I wrestled with my personal identity. I struggled with cultural adaptation. Some of my friends had never heard of samba, Guaraná, or Sonho de Valsa. Americans call "Futebol" soccer (Who came up with the word "soccer" anyway?!). Yet, American Football, which is primarily a game where players use their hands is labeled "Foot-ball." How is that even a thing? Please forgive my little rant ... these were simply my thoughts when I first arrived in America.

I grew up eating white rice and black beans every single day of my life! I constantly thought to myself, "How can Americans miss out on such daily culinary pleasures?" It took me a while to get used to the way people live in America. I was introduced to drinks like Dr. Pepper, Mountain Dew, southern sweet tea, and even learned to appreciate them. Further, I learned the game of American football, which can be quite entertaining once you understand it. I became a big fan of almost all things fast food. What about that dollar menu, huh? I came to love sports like golf, Lacrosse, ultimate frisbee, snow-skiing, and many more.

My life before coming to America was pretty simple. I grew up in a Christian household. I made a conscious personal decision to follow Christ when I was 13 years old. Being a Christ follower is not just part of who I am, it is who I am. But it was only in college that I began to wrestle with the meaning of life and the purpose of my existence.

Coincidently, in the year 2002, Rick Warren published his book *Purpose Driven Life*. That was the year I arrived in the United States. The book seeks to answer the question, "What on earth am I here for?" Spurred by this question I began to ask questions such as: Does my identity equal my upbringing, or something more significant? What role does God play as it relates to my existence? Is the Bible really the Word of God, and if so, what difference should that make to me personally? Why, after learning the Bible and being quite familiar with its contents, did I not realize God's passion and profound love for us as foreigners on this earth? Why did I not realize I was actually born into the world a foreigner? Why was the word foreigner so "foreign" to me?

When I arrived in college, I was soon introduced to the International Club. The International Club was a group for all OBU foreign students to get to know each other. We would hang out and play games, try to decipher what in the world we were trying to say to each other, and occasionally share some amazing (and sometimes, not so amazing) food from our countries. I must admit, I felt really lost at times. Here I was in a foreign country, surrounded by other foreigners from every continent known to man!

Life has been full of excitement. Today, I have lived half of my life in Brazil and half of my life in America. Learning to speak a different language, reasoning, relating, and engaging in new relationships with people from a foreign land is difficult. But, it yields fruit. Today, I am married to a foreigner: my wife Ashli is American, and we have three children who possess dual citizenships. I am now both a citizen of Brazil and America. But neither Brazil nor the United States is my permanent home.

One of the hardest things I had to face when I first arrived in America was fitting in. Let's face it, a square-head person living in a round-headed world will seldom completely fit in. Before I came to America, some of my close friends and family warned me that it would be very hard to form deep relationships with people. American secularism and its hyper-individualistic focus are part of the culture. Like the invisible state lines across the country, it's easy to miss these common realities. Not to mention "personal space," which was such a foreign concept (pun intended) to me, since in my culture people are unapologetically, physically affectionate. What I came to realize over the years, however, is that some things are not necessarily wrong, they are just different.

We are actually all immigrants. Immigration is a hot political topic in America. Most emphasize its negative aspects: illegal immigrants, drug and human trafficking, families being torn apart, disease, and terrorism. Though these issues are important, they are not the purpose of this book. *The purpose of this book is to show that the Bible reveals this world is not our home: instead, we were created to dwell in God's presence and eternal kingdom forever. Until all things are fully made new, we who know Jesus are redeemed-foreigners on earth on mission with God.*

My ideas are framed by a biblical worldview. The term "redeemed-foreigners" does not appear in the Bible. However, throughout the book I argue the idea is there. And in fact, there are many important truths we have from Scripture that are not used in its pages. For instance, terms such as theology, Trinity, Second Coming, Canonical, among others.

Most people are either unaware or simply neglect the fact

that we are all foreigners, temporary citizens on this earth. We are sojourners whose lives were meant for so much more than living in a certain place and time on planet earth. We were created for more than a good education, a family, a good job, and then to retire with a big pension, and finally to die. Is this really the purpose of our existence? My answer is in the negative. We were meant for such much more, and the Bible has the answer.

Hebrews 13:14 in the New Living Translation says, "This world is not our permanent home." Billy Graham once said, "My home is in heaven. I'm just passing through this world." He was right. Our citizenship belongs to a world beyond. We are temporary residents on this earth, not permanent residents, and that is our reality from the moment we are born until the moment that we die (Phil 3:20).

According to the Oxford Dictionary the adjective "permanent" is defined as: lasting or intended to last or remain unchanged indefinitely.[2] The English Oxford dictionary defines immigration as: "The action of coming to live permanently in a foreign country."[3] However, when it comes to our standing before God and the world, our relationship to this world is *not permanent*. God intends for heaven to be our permanent destination. We are only here temporarily. That is why the apostle Paul once wrote, "as we look not to the things that are seen but to the things that are unseen. For the things that are seen are transient, but the things that are unseen are eternal" (2 Corinthians 4:18).

In a nutshell, we are all foreigners and immigrants.

During my college years, I began to dive deeper into God's Word. I began reading the Old and New Testament in a new way. I began learning new things. It was after intensely studying

Scripture that I realized God's love and passion for the nations … all nations!

The evidence is all over the redemptive historical themes of the Bible. It is found in every major section of Scripture (The TANAK [a term that stands for the Law, Prophets, and the Writings, or what we call the Old Testament], the Gospels, Acts, the Epistles, and Revelation, or what we call the New Testament). For instance,

> "Turn to me and be saved, *all the ends of the earth*! For I am God, and there is no other. By myself I have sworn; from my mouth has gone out in righteousness a word that shall not return: To me *every knee* shall bow *every tongue* shall swear allegiance" (Isaiah 45:22–23).

> "Declare his glory among the nations, his marvelous works among all the peoples! For great is the Lord, and greatly to be praised; he is to be feared above all gods" (Psalm 96:3–4).

> "Here is My Servant whom I have chosen, My beloved in whom My soul delights; I will put My Spirit on Him, and He will proclaim justice to the *nations*… The *nations* will put their hope in His name" (Matthew 12:18, 21 NIV).

> "For so the Lord has commanded us, saying, "'I have made you a light for the Gentiles, that you may bring salvation to the ends of the earth'" (Acts 13:47).

> "And they sang a new song, saying, "Worthy are you to take the scroll and to open its seals, for you were slain, and by your blood you ransomed people for God from every tribe and language and people and nation and you have made them a kingdom and priests to our God, and they shall reign on the earth" (Revelation 5:9–10).

We do not choose where to be born. We enter into our earthly existence completely unaware of both its beauty and dangers. We come into the world as foreigners, strangers to an unknown world.

You are a foreigner! We are all foreigners!! Foreigners created in the image of God (Genesis 1:27), longing to be home but still far from it.

The Bible tells us that God created us for his glory (Isaiah 43:7). It also tells us that our citizenship is beyond this world. Through Jesus Christ, believers are transformed from aliens, to redeemed-foreigners, and ultimately to heavenly citizens. We are placed on earth not as permanent aliens, but temporary residents.

This book is divided into two main parts. In part one, I provide the biblical foundation. My goal is to guide you through the Bible to point out the biblical idea that we are all foreigners. Though "foreignness" was not God's initial intent for mankind from the beginning, because of the Fall of mankind in the garden of Eden we are all foreigners. If you appreciate the Bible, you'll enjoy this book. If you are simply someone curious about what the Bible has to teach and say about your life...keep reading!

The Bible is God's revealed words to mankind. It contains his message of love, redemption, and his design for creating us in his image. It reveals our place in his grand narrative. It gives the revelation of God's desire for mankind to dwell in his presence. It shows his glory revealed and understood. My approach is simple: I will attempt to show you what God has communicated throughout Scripture; that we were created to dwell in his presence forever as citizens of his kingdom. Our journey, in part one, begins with the book of Genesis and ends in the book of Revelation.

In this journey I'm going to use a number of terms from the past, such as words from the Hebrew or Greek languages as those were how the Bible was originally copied down. But don't worry, there will be no quiz at the end of the book, and you can still say, 'That's Greek to me!," as the famous expression goes. Or as I used to say, "I no speak English!"

The second part of the book attempts to provide a practical application of the main thrust of the book. It attempts to answer the question, "How shall we then live?" I will explore three main areas in the life of Christian believers (whom I label redeemed-foreigners): family, society, and church. The final three chapters are designed to provide insights on how we should live as redeemed-foreigners while still on earth. Though our time on earth is proportionally insignificant compared to eternity, what we do with our divinely allotted time matters. Those who identify as Christ followers look forward to spending eternity in the presence of God in the afterlife as eternal heavenly citizens. But, until then, what are you and I to do? How are you and I supposed to live? Well, read part two and you'll know!

Who is this book written for?

1. For those who appreciate the Bible
2. For those who like to study God's Word and learn from it
3. For those who would like a fresh perspective in life
4. For those seeking a solid grasp of the Bible's message as it relates to our purpose on this temporary place called earth.

5. For pragmatics seeking to live their earthly lives in a purposeful way

If the above descriptions apply, then I encourage you to journey with me through Scriptures. Keep reading on!

PART ONE

The Biblical Foundation

NO. The "Old" Testament is not the account of "old news." It is not merely a recording of historical accounts of past events. It is not primarily the account of amazing stories of bodies of waters being parted, of angelic appearances, and the people of Israel. It is much more than that. The term "Old Testament" can be misleading. The postmodern person is used to constantly changing news, instant tweets, instant messaging, and new developments in technology, science, and research. Something is "old news" in a matter of days, hours, minutes, and sometimes seconds. If you interact on social media you get this. If you need proof news changes fast, wait a couple of hours and some "breaking news" notification will pop up on your smartphone device or computer screen.

Debates on what the Old Testament should be called are manifold. The term "Old Testament" is used in relation to the New Testament. The word "testament" comes directly from the Latin word *testamentum*, which is a rendition of the Greek word that means "covenant." In the New Testament, Jesus establishes a new *covenant* with his followers. This covenant was predicted in the Old Testament, but only finally realized in the life of Jesus Christ as revealed in the New Testament, the promised Messiah of the Old Testament. This new covenant, which was prophesied throughout the Hebrew Bible (another name for the Old Testament), is clearly announced in Jeremiah 31:31-34:

> "The days are coming," declares the Lord, "when I will make a *new covenant* with the people of Israel and with the people of Judah. It will not be like the *covenant* I made with their ancestors, when I took them by the hand to lead them out of Egypt, because they broke my *covenant*, though I was a husband to them," declares the Lord. "This is the *covenant* I will make with the people of Israel after that time," declares the Lord. "I will put my law in their minds and write it on their hearts. I will be their God and they will be my people. No longer will they teach their neighbor, or say to one another, 'Know the Lord,' because they will all know me, from the least of them to the greatest," declares the Lord. "For I will forgive their wickedness and will remember their sins no more."

Notice the repetition of the word "covenant". This word is used over 280 times in the Hebrew Bible/Old Testament.[4] In the New Testament, when Jesus gathered his disciples before his death, he said, "This is the new *covenant* in my blood, which is poured out for you" (Luke 22:20). This new covenant fulfilled Jeremiah's prophecy.

The first occurrence of the term covenant appears in Genesis 6:18, in the account of the life of Noah: "But I will establish my covenant with you, and you shall come into the ark." Throughout the Hebrew Bible several covenants were made between God and his people. These covenants show the progressive nature of the relationship God established with His people. W. E. Vine writes, "The use of 'Old Testament' and 'New Testament' as the names for the two sections of the Bible indicates that God's 'covenant' is central to the entire book [the Bible]. The Bible relates God's 'covenant' purpose, that man be joined to Him in loving service and know eternal fellowship with Him through the redemption that is in Jesus Christ."[5] A covenant served two purposes: 1) to establish boundaries for obedience, 2) to declare God's intention for a particular person or people through the assurance of a promise.

Though the word covenant does not appear in the Genesis creation account, the idea is there as we see God establishing his first mandate to mankind. God took Adam and put him in a place called the Garden of Eden. He commanded him to "work it and take care of it" (Genesis 2:15). He told him he would be free to eat from any tree in the garden, except one. The fruit of the tree of the knowledge of good and evil was not to be eaten. If humanity chose to eat of it, they would "certainly die" (Genesis 2:17).

The rest of the story is widely known to anyone familiar with the biblical account. Humans did not keep their side of the deal. The covenant God had made with humanity was broken as both man and woman violated his command. They broke the pact God made with them and ate from the tree of the knowledge of good and evil (Genesis 2:16-17; Genesis 3). God's covenant-making activities are his attempt to bring us, foreigners, back into the realm of his dominion. It is his way of repatriating us back into his kingdom and presence.

Basic Covenant Progression

Sinless mankind in Eden (Genesis 1:26-2:3)
Adam and Eve guilty, after sin (Genesis 3:14-19)
Mankind multiplies and becomes further corrupted (Genesis 6)
Noah and his family spared - Noahic Covenant
(Genesis 6:9-8:22)
Noah's sons spread throughout the earth (Genesis 9:8-17)
Abrahamic Covenant (Genesis 12:1-3)
Abraham and the Land of Canaan (Genesis 15:9-21)
Abraham, Circumcision (Genesis 17:1-14)
Abraham, Offspring (Genesis 22:16-18)
Law, Moses and the Israelites - Mosaic Covenant (Exodus 19-24)
Land, Palestinian Covenant (Deuteronomy 30)
David and the Kingdom of Israel (2 Samuel 7:8-19)
New Covenant Announced (Jeremiah 31:31–34)
The Kingdom Proclaimed: John the Baptist (Luke 1:68-78)
Jesus Christ – New Covenant (Matthew 26:28; 16:17-19)
The Church (Acts 2)
Gentiles included (Acts 9-10)
Kingdom and Millennium (Revelation 20)
The New Heavens and the New Earth (Revelation 21)

It is this flow, from Genesis to Revelation, that will be the focus of the first part of this book. We begin with the Hebrew Bible, the Old Testament.

CHAPTER ONE

Foreign Beginnings

"I seek a place that can never be destroyed, one that is pure, and that fadeth not away, and it is laid up in heaven, and safe there, to be given, at the time appointed, to them that seek it with all their heart" – John Bunyan, Pilgrim's Progress

Guess what? I never thought of myself as a foreigner. I always thought other people were foreigners. In my interactions with Argentines, Uruguayans, and Americans growing up, I just thought of them as interesting people, but not as strangers living in a foreign land. Perhaps my youth at the time accounts for my lack of reflection on the subject. Prior to leaving Brazil as a young man, I was not very reflective. But reflecting on the topic of what it means to be a foreigner was on my mind every day from the moment I arrived in America.

I was the first person in my entire family to migrate to the United States. In fact, I was the first one from my immediate family to step foot in North America. Learning new sights and sounds from a foreign place was quite overwhelming. Not to mention trying to communicate in a foreign language I barely knew.

At a basic level most of us associate the word foreigner with someone who is separated from their physical homeland. This is certainly true. However, after I began reflecting on my own reality living in a foreign country, I realized that there are different levels of foreignness: 1) Physical Foreigners: People displaced from their homeland; 2) Spiritual Foreigners: Humanity separated from God by sin; 3) Christian foreigners: Believers in Jesus who serve the Lord on earth but are already citizens of another kingdom, temporary aliens and pilgrims on earth (1 Peter 2:11). It was upon my reflection on the subject in general and a study of the Scriptures in particular that I realized who represented the first foreigners to walk on earth.

Adam And Eve - The First Foreigners

The book of Genesis means "beginning." In the Hebrew language, "genesis" (*bereshit)*, literally means "in the beginning." The Greek Septuagint, the Greek translation of the Hebrew Bible, uses the word *archē*, meaning "origin." In Genesis, you read the account of the origin of the natural world, the creation of mankind in God's image, the forming of civilizations and nations, and God's merciful acts to redeem mankind back to himself after the Fall through Abraham's descendants.

The Bible follows a basic structure. Though many have argued for various ways about its overarching flow, I follow the idea given by Gilbert and DeYoung: "The basic structure of the Bible's narrative seems to unfold in four broad acts: creation, fall, redemption, and consummation."[6] For the purposes of my book, I suggest the following paradigms:

For those who **are** redeemed by God through Jesus Christ:

For those who **are not** redeemed by God through Jesus Christ:

Adam and Eve were the first foreigners to walk on planet earth, because after they sinned against God they were exiled from the garden of Eden, their home. Their account can be found in the first three chapters of the book of Genesis. God created man and woman, male and female, in His image (Genesis 1:27). Why did he do that? To glorify himself! By creating mankind in his image, God established a special relationship between creator and his creation: the possibility for humans to relate to him on a personal level. This is something no other created being on the planet is able to enjoy (Genesis 1:27–28). This relationship was designed to be special. The Scripture tells us that man and woman were allowed to come into the presence of their creator (Genesis 3:8).

God created man and woman to live in perfect harmony with him. He simply asked them to do one thing—NOT to eat from the tree of the knowledge of good and evil. Note, he did not give them an extensive list of do's and don'ts. He simply asked them not to do one thing! And yet they did it! They ate from the fruit of the tree. The consequence: death. Though not immediate, they eventually died physically. However, their spiritual death was immediate.

Before they died physically God did something else. He exiled them! They were cast out from the presence of the Lord, becoming the first foreigners ever in the history of mankind.

> The LORD God said, "Since man has become like one of us, knowing good and evil, he must not reach out, take from the tree of life, eat, and live forever." So, the Lord God *sent him away* from the Garden of Eden to work the ground from which he was taken. *He drove man* [Adam and Eve] *out* and stationed the cherubim and the flaming, whirling sword east of the Garden of Eden to guard the way to the tree of life (Genesis 3:22–24 HCSB).

Man and woman immediately experienced the loss of divine intimacy, and the consequences were not pleasant. Later the Apostle Paul points out that we are separated from God because of our sin. He says we are alienated from God and strangers (foreigners) "having no hope without God in the world" (Ephesians 2:12). Adam is responsible for the chaos that ensued. The words "he sent him away," from the Hebrew root *shalach*, is significant. Adam, who once heard the Lord walking in the garden, was banished from his presence along with his wife, Eve.[7] But even more significant is the use of the verb *garash*, "to drive out." This is a stronger term than "send out," used in v. 22. It is often used in the Pentateuch (the first five books of the Bible, also called the Torah or the Law) of the expulsion of the inhabitants of Canaan (e.g., Exodus 23:28–31). It is coupled with "send out" in Exodus 6:1; 11:1, and in each case it is emphatic. In other words, "God did not just send him forth, an act that would not have precluded all possibility of his returning, but He drove him out—completely."[8]

The word *garash* has a few semantic variations. Among

them: to divorce, to thrust, to cast out, to expel, and to expatriate. The implication is that both Adam and Eve are cast out of their originally intended homeland. The place in which they were born. The place where they had dwelt all of their lives up to that point.[9] Tim Keller writes,

> The story of the human race, however, is one of exile and longing for homecoming. Death and disease have distorted and defaced God's good physical creation. Society is a Babel filled with selfishness, self-exaltation, and pride. Exploitation and violence mar and ruin human community. The world as it now exists is not our true home. We were made for a place without death or parting from love, without decay, and without disease and aging. We are, therefore, exiles and aliens here. Why? Because the human race turned from God to live for itself; our first parents were thrown out of the garden of God and banished from the face of God, in whose presence is our true home.[10]

Interestingly enough, their firstborn son, Cain, was also exiled because of his sin and cursed to wander the earth. The word *garash* also appears in his narrative. Cain pronounced a curse upon himself saying, "behold you have driven me away [*garash*] from the ground" (Genesis 4:14). He predicted he would be a fugitive and wanderer, and wherever he would go people would want to kill him. Not much for a positive life outlook! In conclusion, the first parents and the first children ever to walk on earth became foreigners.

As sin increased upon the earth the sons of man became so corrupt that the Lord decided to exterminate almost all of humanity. It was sort of "reboot" all of creation (Genesis 6–11). Noah was the only found worthy of redemption. He is described as one who walked with God. The Bible tells us he was "a righteous man, blameless among his contemporaries; Noah walked with God" (Genesis 6:9). Through Noah the nations of the earth sprung forth. His sons and their children repopulated the earth. When Noah's genealogy is mentioned the Bible tells us they had formed into nations which spread throughout the earth after the flood (Genesis 10:32).

An interesting turn of events takes place in Genesis 11. At this point all of the nations of the earth spoke the same language; however, in the land of Shinar the Lord confused humanity's language creating stark separation between peoples. It is at the tower of Babel that we see the very first mass immigration event in history. The word Babel means "confusion." The Bible tells us that it was here that God "confused the language of the whole earth" and scattered different peoples throughout the globe (Genesis 11:9). Today we have over 6500 languages and dialects all over the world.

God's intent from the beginning was for all of mankind to live in harmony with him. But we refused him. Our wickedness turned into idolatry, rebellion, and pride beyond imagination. But his mercy triumphed over the judgment humanity deserved, and still deserves, for its sinfulness. God chose a nation from whom he would spring forth salvation.

Illustration by Sara Lynn Miller
Genesis 3:20-24 - "Garden Exiles"

This illustration depicts Adam and Eve as they were being cast out of the garden of Eden. The entrance into Eden was blocked by the flames from the sword held by the cherubim that turned every way to guard the path leading to the tree of life. The symbolism of the crown of thorns holding the art sheds light on the price of forgiveness and loving grace that God gives in Christ, who will one day restore creation back to its Edenic state. The gift of our salvation through God's son, Christ Jesus, and his ultimate sacrifice is woven throughout Scripture from beginning to end.

Abraham The Foreigner

The author of Genesis immediately turns our attention toward Abraham. Abraham, the foreigner. He became a physical foreigner after leaving his earthly homeland, Ur of the Chaldees. He was told to leave his homeland and go to a place where God would send him to make him prosper.

Abraham, or Abram as he was called before the Lord changed his name, is considered the "father" of three of the world's major religions: Judaism, Christianity, and Islam. I remember as a child singing the song titled "Father Abraham." The core of the song is as follows: "Father Abraham had many sons, many sons had Father Abraham, I am one of them and so are you, so let's all praise the Lord." To those who surrender to Christ, Abraham becomes a father figure (Galatians 3:7).

Abraham descended from Shem. Noah blessed Shem after their family exited the ark. The blessing of Shem was merely a foreshadowing of the more significant blessing the Lord would give Abraham in Genesis 12. God was going to make Abraham's name great (Genesis 12:2). Ironically, "Shem" means "name" in the Hebrew language. "Shem is marked for divine blessing and his line is singled out in the subsequent story as a harbinger of hope for the world."[11] Ultimately, one of Abraham's descendants, Jesus, would later in history be given *the name* is above all names:

> Therefore, God has highly exalted him and bestowed on him the *name* that is above every *name*, so that at the *name* of Jesus every knee should bow, in heaven and on earth and under the earth, and every tongue confess that Jesus Christ

is Lord, to the glory of God the Father (Philippians 2:9–11).

But more on that later (chapter 6). Now back to Abraham...

At the tower of Babel, the rebellious builders' main goal was to make a "name" for themselves. They desired to build a tower with its top reaching the heavens. This presumptuous move was driven by their desire to "make a name [sham] for themselves" so they would not be spread throughout the earth (Genesis 11:4).

The nations of the earth had migrated to the land of Shinar, whose ruler was Nimrod, a descendent of Ham, whose offspring God had cursed. Their attempt to make a name for themselves was sinful. Their propensity to stand against God was a blatant rejection of God's rule over mankind. The nations of peoples of the world at that time continued on their quest to replace God with themselves. This self-idolatry is ingrained in the human race. Such idolatry only leads to death. But God intervened.

In the following chapter, Genesis 12, God ensured that mankind understood that he is the only one who is able to make any name great. In Genesis 17, the Lord changed Abram's name to Abraham. Abram means "exalted father." God's desire to make Abram's name great is tied to his seed, or descendants. His descendants would become numerous. Therefore, his name was changed to Abraham, which means "father of many nations."

The promise was intended to reach all nations:

Now the Lord said to Abram, "Go from your country and your kindred and your father's house to the land that I will show you. And I will make of you a great nation, and I will bless you and make your name [*shem*] great, so that you will be a blessing" (Genesis 12:1–2).

In Genesis 12, the Lord sent out Abraham to a foreign land. A land, the Lord says, "that I will show you." This land was Canaan, which became known as the Promised Land because of God's promise to Abraham and his descendants. Abraham was told to become a foreigner physically in a land distant from his own.

I can relate to Abraham's sojourning. I left my own country, family, culture, and context, to go to a country I barely knew. Leaving everything behind can be very difficult. However, if walking by faith means trusting that the Lord has the best in store for you here on earth, what have we to lose? God's promises and his purpose will always be accomplished in our lives when we seek to do his will and walk by faith, no matter where he may send us.

There are two important aspects of God's promise to Abraham in Genesis 12:1–3. First, the Lord promised to bless Abraham and make his name great. And indeed, Abraham became the father of many great nations. Second, the word "blessing" (from the Hebrew root *brk*) occurs five times in these short verses. The first four times the blessing is specifically directed toward Abraham, however the last mention of the word "blessing" in Genesis 12:3 is all-encompassing. Through Abraham, "all" (Hebrew, *kol*) the nations of the earth would be blessed.

Why is this significant? Because it is here that God's plan for Abraham intersects with ours. The adjective "all" is directed toward you and me. God desires for all to be saved (1 Timothy 2:4). So, his promise to bring about our own salvation through Abraham's seed was the plan he chose in order to redeem the world back to himself.

Abraham's life was full of adventure. He sojourned from Mesopotamia to Canaan. Interestingly enough, a famine came over the land of Canaan as soon as Abraham arrived. Then, Abraham and his family became foreigners once again as they headed to Egypt. When in Egypt Abraham lied to Pharaoh about the identity of his wife, Sarah. Abraham showed something all Christians experience throughout their lives, a lapse of faith in God.

Instead of telling the truth, he used deceit to protect himself from harm. This is a dangerous game to play because the consequences can be disastrous. And he did it twice. In Genesis 20, he lied to another king. He committed lies for self-preservation. The biblical narrative gives us insight into Abraham's response to king Abimelech, "Abraham said, 'I did it because I thought, 'There is no fear of God at all in this place, and they will kill me because of my wife'" (Genesis 20:11).

Abraham knew he was a foreign resident wherever he went (Genesis 23:4). One of the greatest fears foreigners have is the fear of not being welcomed. I wonder if he ever wondered why God took him from his homeland and made him a foreigner. Perhaps the Lord wanted him not to forget that this world is not all that the Lord has to offer to his faithful ones. It is easy to forget this world is not our home.

Did Abraham forget God's promise to him? Let's be honest, we often doubt that God's plan and provision will be accomplished. It is part of being human. But how do we prevent ourselves from remaining in this state? I believe the answer lies in "remembrance." Abraham had to be reminded of God's covenant with him in Genesis 15 and 17.

Abraham had just received a promise from the Lord of the

universe! Why did he not trust that God would provide for him? Abraham showed his humanity by succumbing to self-preservation rather than divine provision. We too are subject to such a shortfall. In our attempt toward self-preservation, we forget God's promises. His promise to be with us wherever we go, to not leave us or forsake us, and to guide us to the ultimate Promise Land. To guide us to a place that he is preparing for us.

The words of the song *Amazing Grace* by John Newton are worth remembering:

> The Lord has promised good to me,
> His Word my hope secures
> He will my shield and portion be
> As long as life endures

Although Abraham wavered at times, his faith remained. This is shown most beautifully in Genesis chapter 22 as Abraham, in obedience to the Lord, was willing to sacrifice his own son. Prior to Isaac's near-sacrifice, Abraham and Sarah tried to resolve their offspring's conundrum.

Abraham's behavior was not without consequence.

The main consequence related to his offspring. First, his son Ishmael––who was borne by Sarah's servant, Hagar––was exiled into the wilderness. Notice the word "exiled" (Hebrew, *garash*), is used here just as it was used in Adam's and Cain's story. Like Cain, Ishmael became an exiled, unwanted, and secluded outcast: a foreigner. The only difference between the two is that instead of being cursed, Ishmael is blessed. God promised to make a great nation from Ishmael (Genesis 21:18).

Second, Abraham's son Isaac, who was born miraculously to Sarah, also became a foreigner. His mother Sarah had passed

away. Sarah and Abraham faced many trials in foreig
lived a full life. Sarah died at a ripe old age and so did ᴀ
ham.[12] After Sarah's death, Isaac became a grown man. Fast forward several years later and you read how Isaac committed the
same lying mistake of his father. Like his father and mother, he
tried to escape a famine in the land. Isaac was faced with the
same issue his father had faced back in Egypt, and like his father,
he lied (Genesis 26:7; see Genesis 12:10–20). God then told Isaac
to sojourn (*guwr*), to a land the Lord would tell him. The simi-
larities between Isaac's call and that of his father are striking:

> Now the Lord said to Abram, "Go from your country and
> your kindred and your father's house to *the land that I will
> show you*" (Genesis 12:1).

> And the LORD appeared to him [Isaac] and said, "Do not go
> down to Egypt; dwell in *the land of which I shall tell you*
> (Genesis 26:2).

God's promise to bless Abraham was indeed meant to be a
blessing to all nations (Genesis 17:4). As mentioned above, the
Abrahamic promise was both to blood descendants and to all
who also would become his children through faith. Jason DeR-
ouchie points out, "Genesis 17 envisions a day when Abraham's
'fatherhood' will expand beyond ethnic Israelites to include
the nations."[13]

The crucial role his seed (offspring) played in redemptive
history unfolds throughout God's special revelation (Genesis
22:17b–18; Acts 3:25–26; Galatians 3:14, 16, 29). His seed was
going to be full of foreigners. His descendants would physically live in a land not their own. The Bible records God's own
words to Abraham highlighting their future status as physical

aliens and slaves, "Know for certain that your offspring will be sojourners [or "foreigners," Hebrew, *guwr*] in a land that is not theirs" (Genesis 15:13). Later we see this prophecy fulfilled as the Israelites become foreigners in Egypt. In fact, God told Abraham that his offspring would become *foreigners* and then be enslaved for 400 years. It is here that we turn our attention to another foreigner named Jacob, Abraham's grandson.

Jacob The Foreigner

Isaac, like Abraham, had become a physical foreigner. It is no surprise that Jacob and Esau, the sons of a foreigner, also became foreigners. Jacob was a man whose life was not devoid of much controversy, sojourning, and trials. His trials were foretold to his mother, Rebecca, at his birth. God appointed him to rule over his older brother:

> And the Lord said to her, "Two nations are in your womb,
> and two peoples from within you shall be divided; the
> one shall be stronger than the other, the older [Esau]
> shall serve the younger [Jacob]" (Genesis 25:23).

Fast-forward a few years. Jacob and Esau became grown men. Jacob, to whom Isaac did not intend to bless at first, impersonated his brother Esau in order to deceive his father into giving him the family blessing. Isaac's blessing to his son Jacob echoes the themes found in Abraham's blessing of land, and the covenantal pattern of blessing and cursing. This blessing mirrored the blessing God previously given:

> And Isaac smelled the smell of his garments and blessed

him and said,

> "See, the smell of my son
> is as the smell of a field that the Lord has blessed!
> May God give you of the dew of heaven
> and of the fatness of the earth
> and plenty of grain and wine.
> Let peoples serve you,
> and nations bow down to you.
> Be lord over your brothers,
> and may your mother's sons bow down to you.
> Cursed be everyone who curses you,
> and blessed be everyone who blesses
> you!" (Genesis 27:27–29).

Esau hated Jacob and wanted to kill him. Echoes of Cain and Abel's story resound throughout this narrative. Because of this family feud, Jacob fled to a foreign land. Jacob's deceit turned him into a foreigner in Mesopotamia. There he married two of his mother's nieces, Leah and Rachel. His family grew, and eventually he returned to Canaan (Genesis 33:18).

The Bible tells us that Jacob's wives worshipped foreign idols. As a matter of fact, Rachel, prior to leaving her homeland, stole her fathers' foreign idols to take with her to Canaan with Jacob and the rest of his family. These foreign idols corrupted Jacob's family. It is here that we see how easily it is to turn to false idols if we are not careful.

Jacob's story is similar to many Christian immigrants today. I remember when I left Brazil and realized that I was completely removed from my parents, church, friends, and culture. Everything that I had learned was challenged. Was I just a Christian because my parents raised me in a Southern Baptist Church? Was I truly a Christ follower, fully devoted, and committed to the gospel? I was challenged morally, emotionally, and most definitely spiritually!

Temptations were plentiful. Though my parents did everything they could to instill in me proper cultural, familial, and moral values, my spiritual resolve was put to the test. I am certain Jacob went through the same difficult challenge. He had to make a choice whether or not to follow God. His wives did also since they were raised in a pagan environment. Jacob must have struggled with which "god" to serve. Would he serve the God of his fathers or would he bow down to his wives' foreign idols? Would he serve the God of his fathers, the God of the universe? The God of Abraham and Isaac?

The idols of this world can easily turn us away from God. They appeal to our materialistic and prideful nature. We can touch and manipulate them in whichever way we want. But the living God cannot be easily manipulated. Jacob, thankfully, realized his mistake. He ordered his family to get rid of the *foreign idols* that had corrupted them. Jacob's orders were a type of family cleansing. They purified themselves of all idolatry before heading to Bethel and worshipped the Lord by building an altar as a sign of consecration (Gen 35:2–3). Jacob recognized God had been faithful to him, and now it was his family turn to be faithful to God.

If there is one thing for which we must all be reminded is that God, as it was in Jacob's case, is with us everywhere we go. God can physically move you to a foreign country, but one thing is for sure, he accompanies you in your journey. The question you have to answer is: Am I going to recognize he is with me, or will I turn away to other false idols like money, power, people, or worldly things that so easily replace godly affection?

Joseph, The Foreigner

Joseph was the son of a foreigner, and he also became a foreigner. Are you beginning to see the pattern? The account of Joseph's life and his kin is one of Scripture's most dramatic and fascinating stories. He is first introduced in Genesis 37. What is interesting is that the story plot of the Genesis narrative highlighting the life of Joseph begins with these verses:

> Jacob lived in the land of his father's *sojournings*, in the land of Canaan. These are the generations of Jacob. Joseph, being seventeen years old, was pasturing the flock with his brothers. He was a boy with the sons of Bilhah and Zilpah, his father's wives. And Joseph brought a bad report of them to their father (Genesis 37:1–2).

Notice that Jacob's father, Isaac, is mentioned as a stranger, a sojourner, or a foreigner (*maguwr*). Ironically (or perhaps purposefully), most of Joseph's story unfolded while he was a foreigner, a stranger, in a land far from his own, the land of Egypt.

Joseph's story is full of twists and turns. Joseph's band of brothers betrayed him, selling him to an Ishmaelite caravan, which was headed to Egypt. And they lied to their father, saying Joseph died. While in Egypt Joseph became a slave. He was not only a foreigner, but he was also a slave! It is one thing to come into a country by your own personal choice, it is a totally different thing to be sent to a place as a slave and live as a slave.

Though Joseph's story was not off to a great start, the Bible interjects throughout the narrative that greater things were in store for this young man. The text tells us that he "became a successful man." His prosperity was God-given, because his master "saw the Lord was with him and caused all that he did to succeed in his hands" (Genesis 39:2-3). The young man mesmerized everyone around him (Genesis 39:4). The Lord was with Joseph and extended kindness to him. First, he blessed him in Potiphar's house.

Despite being thrown in jail unjustly (Genesis 39), God granted him favor in the eyes of the prison warden. The warden put all the prisoners who were in the prison under Joseph's authority. Joseph became responsible for everything that was done there. The warden did not bother with anything under Joseph's authority, *"because the Lord was with him,"* and the Lord made everything that he did successful (Genesis 39:21-23). Even the Pharaoh of Egypt, after encountering Joseph for the first time, recognized the Lord was with Joseph. And Pharaoh said to his servants, "Can we find a man like this, in whom is the Spirit of God?"(Genesis 41:37-8).

I wonder if Joseph "felt" that the Lord was truly with him. Could you imagine being a foreigner and slave in a distant land? Could you imagine winding up in jail with no prospect of a bright future? While waiting for deliverance from imprisonment, Joseph must have certainly felt neglected and alone. He was sold into slavery at age 17, spent years in jail, and did not become second in all Egypt to Pharaoh until he was 30 years old (see Genesis 37:2; 41:46). Yet Joseph the foreigner was blessed by God.

The text shows the reader that Joseph excelled wherever he went because the Lord was with him. He was put in charge of Potiphar's household, he was put in charge of all the prisoners while in prison, and finally he received the ultimate reward:

he was put in charge of Egypt's entire kingdom. Joseph is an example of what we should be like as foreigners. Here's a list of things we can learn from Joseph the foreigner:

1. We should seek to walk with and honor God wherever he sends us.
2. We must not let our present circumstances determine our final outcome.
3. We should honor others wherever we go.
4. We must be patient and wait for the Lord's promised deliverance and not rush to try to fulfill them on our own.
5. We must understand that the Lord is with us wherever we go.

Too often we set our agenda and our plans and ask God to bless them. This seems like a spiritual act, but it's actually very selfish. It's far better to surrender our lives to God's plan and spend more energy hearing from him than getting him to affirm our own plans. After Joseph was put in charge of Egypt, the great famine he predicted via Pharaoh's dream, struck the land. The story takes an interesting turn. His brothers, who had sold him as a slave, traveled to Egypt in need of relief. When they arrived in Egypt Joseph encountered them. Interestingly, Joseph determined to treat his brothers as foreigners (from the Hebrew *nekar*), using a harsh tone with them at first (Genesis 42:7). Do you blame him? Joseph was human after all and this was an emotional encounter.

Do you see the irony? His brothers, foreigners in Egypt, came to beg him for mercy. Joseph did not automatically reveal his identity. What is fascinating is that they did not even recognize him when they saw him face to face. The text tells us that

Joseph "pretended to be a foreigner." The account of Joseph's life and sojourning is one of the most riveting in all Scripture (Genesis 37–50). Eventually, the brothers who sold him into slavery were forgiven. After they made amends, Jacob's sons, by the providence of God through Joseph were able to settle as foreigners in Egypt.

Joseph the foreigner was used by God to save the descendants of Abraham, Isaac, and Jacob. He indeed was blessed. In fact, Joseph lived to be 147 years old!! The Lord used a foreigner to save other foreigners. His brothers became foreigners and settled in Egypt for the rest of their lives. Hundreds of years later, the Israelites became a multitude of foreigners!

CHAPTER TWO

"Alien-nation"

"The sweetest thing in all my life has been the longing—to reach the Mountain, to find the place where all the beauty came from—my country, the place where I ought to have been born. Do you think it all meant nothing, all the longing? The longing for home? For indeed it now feels not like going, but like going back" – C.S. Lewis, Till We Have Faces

Guess what? Foreigners more often than not feel alienated; they feel foreign! I experienced this firsthand when I came to live in America. People made fun of my accent, struggled to include me in their circle of friends, and treated me differently because of my background. I must admit, I felt alienated from society. I only had a few friends to hang out with, mostly missionary kids who grew up in my country.

I remember taking ESL (English as a Second Language) classes with a group of foreign students and thinking to myself, "Wow, this is a diverse bunch." We all felt like aliens living in a foreign land, because that is exactly who we were. We were strangers in a foreign land struggling to fit in; most of us did not even understand each other half of the time. The struggle to fit in was real.

Each of us can experience alienation spiritually, emotionally, and relationally. Spiritually, we can feel distant from God because we are overwhelmed trying to fit into society and can easily neglect our hearts. Often spiritual alienation leads to an existential crisis which can wreck your life. Emotionally, foreigners feel alienated because no one is able to understand their issues fully and often fail to express empathy. Relationally, foreigners are typically the odd ones out. I remember people calling me "buddy" while calling their friends "bro" or "dude," placing me in a different relational category. I'm not writing cathartically; this is simply how life was for me while settling in America as a college student.

The Israelites also felt the struggles of alienation. Jacob, or Israel, as God renamed him (Genesis 35:10), had his twelve sons and their descendants settle in Egypt for hundreds of years. It was there that this small family of foreigners became a multitude. The book of Exodus names each of Jacob's sons and proceeds to tell us the Israelites were fruitful and greatly increased in numbers. In fact, the Bible points out they "multiplied and grew exceedingly strong and the land was filled with them" (Exodus 1:7). This terminology is the same used in Genesis 1:28 when God spoke to Adam and Eve, which points to the redemptive plan of God to bring about the salvation of humanity from the Israelites.

The sons of Israel, which is a more literal translation of Exodus 1:7, established themselves as a "people," or a *nation* in Egypt. Here the author seems to want to communicate that they are no longer a small family, but a nation. This nation was the seed of Abraham. Through Jacob's sons the Israelites finally became a people, a people chosen and set apart for God. They became an alien nation. Their vast numbers posed a problem for the ruler of Egypt, the Pharaoh.

Enter Moses.

Moses The Foreigner

After years of prosperity in the land of Egypt, the tables were turned against the Israelites. One of Egypt's foreign rulers, a Pharaoh who came after Joseph's time, oppressed and enslaved them. However, in a dramatic turn of events, God preserved the life of a small child named Moses. Drama is par for the course in the Bible. This Hebrew child through God's providential hand wound up in the hands by Pharaoh's own daughter and was raised by her!

Moses grew up among the privileged. However, as an adult he came face to face with the strenuous reality of his people. One day he took matters into his own hands. He saw an Egyptian beating an Israelite. Moses killed the Egyptian and buried him, thinking no one saw. But Pharaoh learned of it and sought to kill Moses (see Exodus 2:11–15). Like Simba in the *Lion King*, Moses fled for his life, in his case to the land of Midian. The Midianites thought he was an Egyptian. After all, he was raised by Egyptians, dressed, and spoke like an Egyptian. He had fully assimilated into Egyptian culture.

Like his forefathers, Moses became a foreigner in a distant land from his upbringing. In this new foreign land, he married Zipporah. She birthed him a son. Moses also thought of himself as a foreigner. This is made explicit by the name he gives his firstborn, Gershom. Moses gave him this name because, in how own words, "I have been a sojourner in a foreign land" (Exodus

2:21–22).

The writer gives us a pun in the original language, though you can't see it in English versions. "Gershom" is a form of *gur* ("stranger") and comes from the terms *gur* plus *sham* ("sojourn" plus "there"). So, the name is connected with "stranger" and "there," an explanation that connects it with both Moses' past and his new situation. The foreign land to which Moses refers must be understood to be Egypt, not Midian. Egypt, the place of Moses' birth, was never home. There, Moses was a stranger, no matter how familiar the land and the ways of its people had become.[14]

Moses spent a large portion of his life (40 years) tending sheep in the wilderness of Midian, so he was somewhat familiar with living in a deserted land.[15] Moses, the surrogate son of Pharaoh, a royal prince, a learned man, had settled in a foreign land devoid of the comforts of the palace of the most powerful nation in the world at that time. He became a shepherd. The comforts, which he once enjoyed, were replaced by a lowly life of herding sheep in the desert for some forty years.

Moses grew up among foreigners and later became a foreigner in the land of Midian. He, like Joseph, had no prospects for a bright future. But God had something else planned for him. His sojourning to a distant and foreign land was only the precursor to the mighty deeds the Lord would perform through him. After the Lord appeared to Moses he returned to Egypt. Upon his return Moses was 80 years old (Exodus 7:7). Eighty years old? That's right, he was an old man.

God was faithful to the covenant he made with Moses' forefathers. After they grew in Egypt, he reminded Moses of who they were. He reminded Moses that his forefathers were foreigners, just like him. He tells Moses, "I also established my covenant with them to give them the land of Canaan, the land in which they lived as sojourners [foreigners]" (Exodus 6:4).

After a series of miraculous events, Moses finally led the Israelites out of Egypt, because the Lord is a redeeming God. The journey was harsh. The Israelites complained and at times wished they had stayed in Egypt rather than being freed from slavery. As the saying goes, "You can take the kid out of the country, but you can't take the country out of the kid." The biblical text informs us of the many complaints the Israelites had on their way to the Promised Land. The Torah records their grumbling and complaining:

1. They grumbled when they left Egypt and were stopped in front of the Red Sea – Exodus 14:11-12
2. They grumbled and complained against God and Moses for lack of the provision of water – Exodus 15:22-25
3. They grumbled and complained against God and Moses for the lack of food – Exodus 16:1-3
4. They targeted their grumbling specifically against God himself! – Exodus 16:8
5. They also targeted their grumbling against Moses – Exodus 17:3-4

Let's take pause and briefly examine the first account of the Israelites grumbling in the desert:

When Pharaoh drew near, the people of Israel lifted up their eyes, and behold, the Egyptians were marching after them, and they feared greatly. And the people of Israel cried out to the Lord. They said to Moses, "Is it because there are no graves in Egypt that you have taken us away to die in the wilderness? What have you done us in bringing us out of Egypt? Is not this what we said to you in Egypt: 'Leave us alone that we may serve the Egyptians'? For it would have been better for us to serve the Egyptians than to die in the wilderness (Exodus 14:10–12).

One of the most powerful forces of change in the universe is fear. One of the biggest causes of fear is that we forget. How quickly the Israelites forgot God's miraculous deliverance. Lest we be too hard on them, it's easy for us to do the same, right? This is why gratitude helps us to remember God's goodness.

The Israelites, who had been in captivity for centuries, had just experienced the miraculous and extraordinary acts of God against their oppressors as he decimated not only the Egyptian people but also their land. The exodus from Egypt was dramatic, miraculous, and filled with awesome acts. However, when they found themselves cornered by their oppressors one last time, instead of fully trusting God, they complained instead! As the text shows us, they did not want God, they wanted to go back to Egypt! They soon leveled Moses, the Lord's chosen one, to be blamed for their misfortunes.

Could you imagine being Moses? I currently serve on staff that leads a congregation of about 3000 people. I hear complaints on a regular basis, and I'm not even the senior pastor! Most senior pastors hear complaints every single week, sometimes every single day depending on their context. Now, can you imagine having over a million people complaining to you? Can you imagine the stress and weight on Moses' shoulders?

The Israelites' trust in God waned as quickly as it came. Part of our challenge in living in this world (which is not our permanent home) is that we are far too easily intimidated by worldly challenges. Let's be honest, it is very difficult to stay composed and remain steadfast when life is filled with constant trials. However, we must be resolute in our endeavor to remain faithful to the Lord and wait for his supernatural deliverance. Though the trials of this world are often enormous, God's heavenly provision is exponentially more glorious!

The Israelites, like us, had a lot to learn. Moses faithfully led them through the wilderness for 40 years (Numbers 32:13). They turned into grumbling foreigners, even after God tried to lead them into the Promised Land. His goal all along was to dwell in their midst. That is why he established a dwelling among them, the tabernacle. The tabernacle was constructed in a way that was intended to point back toward Eden where there was perfect fellowship with God, but they seemed not to understand it.   And it was in the wilderness that they would learn God's own parameters for a nation whom he chose to be holy unto him (see Exodus 19:4–6).

The Israelites - Foreigners Among Foreigners

The Israelites were familiar with living as foreigners. As a matter of fact, they also had foreigners among them when they exited out of Egypt. Not everyone among the Israelites who fled Egypt was a Hebrew.

> And the people of Israel journeyed from Rameses to Succoth, about six hundred thousand men on foot, besides women and children. A **mixed multitude** also went up with them, and very many livestock, both flocks and herds (Exodus 12:37–38).

Thus, from the outset of their journey, the Israelites had other foreigners among them. Their society was composed of certain foreigners. In fact, God included certain laws to protect the foreigner in the Sinai covenant. Regulations concerning foreigners were given, and they were to be kept, because God cared about the oppressed and the stranger among his people. This served to remind the Israelites of two things: 1) that they too were foreigners, and 2) that all foreigners were created in the *imago Dei*.

The promise given to Abraham was not exclusive to Israel alone. The Israelites had to learn to treat their neighbors as themselves. When Jesus summarized the Law in the Old Testament, he was clear: Love God, love others (see Matthew 22:37–39). No conditions added. And this also applies toward loving those who are considered foreigners among us.

Growing up life seemed very homogeneous. I never stopped to think about what it means to be a foreigner. Many of us think that everyone is just like us when we are younger. Even though while growing up I had friends who were Japanese, African, and Argentinian, I never reflected on what it means to be a foreigner until I became one. I remember from time to time an older Sikh gentleman who walked around my grandmother's neighborhood wearing his *dastaar* (a turban worn by Sikh men). How easy it is for us to assume there are no foreigners among us. How easy it is for us to live our lives ignorant of other people groups, even if they are our neighbors. How easy it is for us to elevate our own heritage without valuing others' properly. How easy it is for us to forget we too are foreigners.

The Torah gives us a precise glimpse into God's heart for the foreigner. Foreigners were to be treated fairly, neighborly, and lovingly:

> When a stranger sojourns with you in your land, you shall not do him wrong. You shall treat the stranger who sojourns with you as the native among you, and you shall love him as yourself, for you were strangers in the land of Egypt: I am the Lord your God (Leviticus 19:33–34).

Note that the Israelites were to treat the foreigner well because God saved them from slavery in Egypt, when they too were foreigners. As it related to having slaves in their midst, God said:

> He executes justice for the fatherless and the widow, and loves the sojourner, giving him food and clothing. Love the sojourner [foreigner], therefore, for you were sojourners [foreigners] in the land of Egypt (Deuteronomy 10:18–19).

Foreigners were also to be treated with respect,

> You shall have the same rule for the sojourner and for the native, for I am the Lord your God (Leviticus 24:22).

As it related to foreign nations they came into contact with:

> You shall not abhor an Edomite, for he is your brother. You shall not abhor an Egyptian, because you were a sojourner [foreigner] in his land (Deuteronomy 23:7).

In the context of Deuteronomy 15, the Israelites are told that the needy and the poor would always be among them. This is a blatant reference to foreigners. The poor in the land were not to be despised. God instructed his people saying, "open wide your hand to your brother, to the needy and to the poor" (Deuteronomy 15:11). The idea behind an open hand versus a closed fist evokes the idea of generosity.

Notice the posture God commanded his people to have toward this section of society. The Hebrew word used here is *tsavah*, which means to "give charge to" or "ordered to." God wanted to make sure the Israelites knew his desired treatment of foreigners was not a suggestion, but a directive. Not an indicative, but an imperative.

A good portion of the population of any nation is composed primarily of immigrants. Most of these are of low-income. For instance, in 2012 the Bureau of Labor Statistics, of the United States Department of Labor reported:

> In 2012, there were 25 million foreign-born persons ages 16 years and older in the U.S. labor force, representing 16.1 percent of the total. About 130 million workers were native born, making up the remaining 83.9 percent of the total U.S. labor force. About 38 percent (9.5 million workers) of the foreign born were from Mexico and Central America, and 28 percent (7 million workers) were from Asia (including the Middle East). The share of foreign–born workers from Europe and the Caribbean was about 10 percent for each.[16]

What do we do with this information? Like the Israelites, we must not forget the stranger among us. We also need to ensure our immigration laws are fair and balanced. Further, believers need to welcome strangers into their homes and lives (more on this in part 2).

"In-Alien-Able " Rights

All human beings have intrinsic value. This value was given to us by God. All people were created in God's image, no matter their place of birth. The founders of America recognized this reality. They believed all persons are born with inalienable rights. Inalienable rights are,

Personal rights held by an individual which are not bestowed by law, custom, or belief, and which cannot be taken or given away, or transferred to another person, are referred to as 'inalienable rights.' The U.S.Constitution recognized that certain universal rights cannot be taken away by legislation, as they are beyond the control of a government, being naturally given to every individual at birth, and that these rights are retained throughout life … The Declaration of Independence gives three examples of inalienable rights, in the well-known phrase, "Life, Liberty, and the Pursuit of Happiness." These fundamental rights are endowed on every human being by his or her Creator and are often referred to as "natural rights."[17]

The founders of America gave testament to the *imago Dei*. God wanted the Israelites to understand they too needed to treat foreigners with respect because of their intrinsic value. In this way, God wanted his people to know all people were created in his image and need to be respected. A person's status as a foreigner does not diminish the *imago Dei*.

Foreigners lived among the Israelites, but who was considered a foreigner? In the Hebrew Bible, according to S. Barabas, "A 'non-citizen,' is roughly equivalent to an 'alien' dwelling in a country either as a temporary guest, perhaps for purposes of trade, or as a permanent resident alien. The three Hebrew words which refer to foreigners are translated in a variety of ways – foreigner, alien, stranger, sojourner – and are practically indistinguishable in meaning."[18] He points out the word "foreigner," and its equivalents, was applied not only to non-Israelites residing in Palestine more or less permanently, but also to Israelites making their home for a time in other lands (Genesis 23:4; 26:3; 47:4; Exodus 2:22; Ruth 1:1)." He further elaborates,

There was one law for the foreigner and the native (Exod. 12:49; Lev. 24:22), and in legal actions they were entitled to the same justice as the Israelites (Deut. 1:16) and were liable to the same penalties (Lev. 20:2; 24:16, 22). Israelites were warned not to oppress foreigners, since they themselves were once strangers in the land of Egypt (Exod. 22:21; 23:9; Lev. 19:33, 34). Foreigners were to be loved and treated like native Israelites (Lev. 19:34; Deut. 10:19), for God loves them (Deut. 10:18) and watches over them (Psa. 146:9; Mal. 3:5).[19]

The Israelites had foreigners living among them in the wilderness. They followed them into the Promised Land. Soon after their journey in the wilderness, the Israelites, who were foreigners in Egypt, would be received as foreigners in the land of their forefathers.

CHAPTER THREE

Foreigners in the Promised Land

"Life is a journey, not a home; a road, not a city of habitation; and the enjoyments and blessings we have are but little inns on the roadside of life, where we may be refreshed for a moment, that we may with new strength press on to the end - to the rest that remaineth for the people of God"
– Horatius Bonar

Guess what? I thought--as so many do--that America was the Promised Land. Growing up in the eighties and nineties was a lot of fun. As a teenager in Brazil my life was filled with American pop culture: American rap music, break dancing, Hollywood movies, American fashion, and so much more. At the age of 14 I was a proud owner of a Charlotte Hornets hat with a metal logo of the team's mascot. I thought it was the coolest hat on earth and I wore it proudly.

Fast forward several years to the time I received a scholarship to study in the American Promised Land. By the grace of God, I succeeded in my college studies. I also met my wife Ashli in college, and we've been married over almost fifteen years now. We have three beautiful sons and God has allowed us to prosper, for which we give him praise. The journey has not been easy, but it has been rewarding!

America was for me, and still is for so many, a sort of Promised Land for foreigners. Today, people risk traveling across the world to live in America. People risk their lives to cross the U.S.-Mexico border. But every Promised Land has its challenges. People live in the Promised Land, after all, and people can be difficult. Life is often harder than expected even in the Promised Land. Both the journey to and life in the Promised Land brings unexpected challenges.

The Israelites experienced hardships as they traveled to and arrived in the Promised Land. Upon Moses' death, God appointed Joshua as his replacement. Joshua was a faithful servant to Moses (Exodus 17:9). In fact, he was Moses' assistant and started serving him at a young age. In other words, ever since the escape of the Israelites from Egypt, Joshua traveled with Moses wherever he went. He, like Moses, was a foreigner. His role as the "new Moses" is highlighted in the book of Joshua.

Joshua was tasked with leading God's people into the Promised Land. And indeed, he did. James Hamilton points out, "Under Joshua, Israel entered the Promised Land, passing by the angel with the flashing sword and through the waters of Jordan to conquer the Canaanites and enjoy God's presence in a new Eden. Like Adam in the first Eden, the nation failed, rebelled, and was exiled from God's presence."[20] His goal was to enter the land, conquer it, and establish settlement in a new land for God's people. Eventually, however, they fail, but more on that later.

Although they entered the land of their ancestors, the Israelites came into the land as foreigners. Foreign nations they encountered were afraid of them (i.e., Joshua 2:8–11; 5:1). God purposed his people to destroy certain wicked pagan nations.

The Canaanites, Hittites, Hivites, Perizzites, Girgashites, Amorites, and Jebusites were to be driven out of the land by the Israelites.

The first challenge confronting the Israelites was the city of Jericho. Before setting foot in the Promised Land, Joshua sent a couple of spies to scout the land. They entered the city and there came into contact with a foreigner. Her name was Rahab. She was a prostitute who lived in the city of Jericho (Joshua 2:1). God used Rahab, a foreigner, to accomplish his plan. This foreigner was a God-fearer, and God used her mightily. The Bible tells us the people of Jericho feared the Israelites as if their hearts had "melted" and as if deadly fear had come over them. But Rahab's assertion as to why they felt that way is what is most revealing about her faith, she said, "for the Lord your God, he is God in the heavens above and on the earth beneath" (Joshua 2:11).

Rahab the foreigner holds a special place in God's redemptive plan. She was a foreigner who helped God's people in their first conquest inside the Promised Land. After the destruction of Jericho, she became a foreign immigrant among the Israelites (Joshua 6:25). Rahab is later mentioned in Christ's genealogy in the book of Matthew, among two other foreigners, Ruth and Tamar (Matthew 1:1–5; Hebrews 11:31 and James 2:25).

What is fascinating about Rahab is that the author of the book of Joshua indicates she feared Yahweh. Rahab had faith in the Lord of the people of Israel. Her lifestyle was certainly immoral. The Bible does not tell us how she fell into such disgrace. It is also likely she left prostitution after the Jericho conquest. Most importantly, what is highlighted is her faith in Yahweh. Her faith is contrasted by the lack of faith of God's people.

After the Israelites conquered Jericho, they fought many battles. They defeated foreign nations and established themselves in Canaan even though their peace was never fully realized. Joshua chapters 23–24 recount their story. After Joshua became very old (Joshua 23:1–2), he challenged the nation of Israel to remain steadfast in their commitment to God. He does four things:

> 1. He reminds them that God fights for them and will continue to if they remain obedient (Joshua 23:3–4).
>
> 2. He encourages them to remain faithful to God, like he was when he took over Moses' leadership (Joshua 1:8; 23:6):
>
> 3. He warns them of the consequences of idolatry to foreign gods and disobedience (Joshua 23:7–8 and 16).
>
> 4. He also cautions them not to intermarry with foreigners from the nations they fought against, because they would corrupt them (Joshua 23:12–13).

Joshua knew that the Israelites would be tempted to fall into idolatry. He knew they were prone to turn to false gods. He pleaded with them to forsake corruption from the foreign pleasures they were going to be exposed to. Further, he knew God is a just God who punishes evil and sin. That is why he wrote, "If you forsake the Lord and serve *foreign* gods, he will turn and bring disaster on you and make an end of you, after he has been good to you." Oftentimes foreign things, worldly things, replace our devotion to God.

Even though the Israelites remained faithful to God during

Joshua's lifetime, their devotion waned. The saga and consequences of their rebellion is blatantly shown in the accounts described in the book of Judges.

Foreign Peoples, Foreign Gods, And Chaos

The Israelites' failure to drive out foreign nations from the Promise Land yielded catastrophic consequences. The Israelites never succeeded in completely expelling the foreign idolatrous peoples who lived in the land of Canaan. Joshua 13:13 records the failure of God's people by highlighting the fact that the Israelites did not expel the Geshurites and Maachathites, who dwelt in Canaan from the land. And this is just one example of their lack of resolve.

The Book of Judges magnifies their fecklessness. The various tribes of Israel succumbed to temptation. Their obedience to God was short-lived. Abraham, Isaac, and Jacob must have been rolling in their graves during this period of time. Though God desired to be their king, they were often ruled and oppressed by foreigners. Why? Because they "did evil in the sight of the Lord and served the Baals [foreign gods]" (Judges 2:11). God had redeemed, delivered, and performed miracles among his chosen nation. All he asked in return was obedience. But their devotion was floundering.

Judges 2:12–13 uses strong language to describe their apostasy, by pointing out that they "abandoned" the Lord, sought after other gods, especially the gods of the Canaanites by bowing down to them. Their abandonment of the Lord provoked his anger. The Hebrew word for "abandoned" (`azab) is the same word God spoke to his people in Deuteronomy 31:6

and Joshua 1:5 assuring them he would never abandon or forsake them:

> Be strong and courageous. Do not fear or be in dread of them, for it is the LORD your God who goes with you. He will not leave you or *forsake* you (Deuteronomy 31:6).

To be clear, God kept his pact. He was faithful to his people and promises, even though they abandoned him. Note that God promised he would "not" forsake his people. But the Israelites did not keep their part of the deal. Rather, they worshipped the gods of the foreign nations among them. The Lord foretold to Moses the people would "whore after" foreign gods (Deuteronomy 31:16).

The Israelites were predicted to "whore" after foreign gods. Such strong language serves to highlight the gravity of their sin. The book of Judges is the fulfillment of this prophetic word against the Israelites. They indeed forsook and broke God's covenant.

The book of Judges follows a cycle of apostasy that can be summarized this way (Judges 2:10–19):

Israelites Serving God

Israelites Delivered

Israelites Do Evil

The Cycle
of Judges

**God Provides a
Rescuer/Judge**

Slavery and War

Israelites Cry Out to God

Israel was enslaved and oppressed because of their sin. Why? Because foreign idolatry lured them into transgression. One of the biggest challenges for God's people during that time, and even today, is misplaced worship.

The world's sensuality appeals to the desires of our flesh. Further, mankind's urge to control, its search for self-fulfillment, and pride, are antithetical to service to God. There are a few reasons the Israelites fell into idolatrous sin: 1) the nations around them served other gods, 2) they were used to seeing gods made by human hands like the Baals and Ashtaroth, 3) the rituals of pagan religions involved sexual acts, and 4) pagan gods were easy to manipulate. However, the greatest reason was that their urges, feelings, and cravings (like ours) were too weak. C. S. Lewis puts it this way,

> It would seem that Our Lord finds our desires not too strong, but too *weak*. We are half-hearted creatures, fooling about with drink and sex and ambition when infinite joy is offered us, like an ignorant child who wants to go on making mud pies in a slum because he cannot imagine

what is meant by the offer of a holiday at the sea. *We are far too easily pleased.*[21]

The period of the Judges lasted for over 300 years. The one theme of the book is that "Israel did evil in the eyes of the Lord" (Judges 2:11; 3:7; 4:1; 6:1; 10:6; 13:1). In fact, the last verse of the book states, "In those days there was no king in Israel. Everyone did what was right in their own eyes" (Judges 21:25). Israel had many judges during this period of history. However, the lawlessness of God's people is most vividly represented in the person of Samson.

Judges 13 highlights the terms of Samson's birth. He was chosen to be set apart from birth as a Nazarite. He was set apart, like the Israelites were by God. Samson's life and saga highlight the very tale of God's people. They too defiled themselves, sought after pagan women, rituals, and practices. Samson did not want to be an Israelite, he wanted to be a foreigner. He lusted after foreign women. He took a wife from among the Philistines (Judges 14:1–3). He mingled among foreigners (Judges 14:10–14). He was seduced by a foreign prostitute named Delilah (Judges 16:1–5). He was enslaved and tortured by foreigners (Judges 16:20–21), and ultimately died as a foreigner among foreigners (Judges 16:23–30).

The consequence of foreign corruption in the midst of Israel led to years of oppression in the land. Below is a chart that offers a timeline of the book of Judges and the various events of those days:

THE JUDGES

Judge	Biblical Reference	Judges Tribes	Foreign Oppressor	Years of Oppression	Years of Rest	Total Length of Rule
Othniel	3:7–11	Judah	Mesopotamia	8 years (3:8)	40 years (3:11)	48 years
Ehud	3:12–30	Benjamin	Moab	18 years (3:14)	80 years (3:30)	98 years
Shamgar	3:31		Philistines			
Deborah	Chapters 4–5	Ephraim	Canaan	20 years (4:3)	40 years (5:31)	60 years
Gideon	Chapters 6–8	Manasseh	Midian	7 years (6:1)	40 years (8:28	47 years
Tola	10:1–2	Issachar			23 years (10:2	23 years
Jair	10:3–5	Gilead-Manasseh			22 years (10:3)	22 years
Jephthah	10:6–12:7	Gilead-Manasseh	Ammonites		24 years (10:8;12:7)	24 years
Ibzan	12:8–10	Judah or Zebulun			7 years (12:9)	7 years
Elon	12:11–12	Zebulun			10 years (12:11)	10 years
Abdon	12:13–15	Ephraim			8 years (12:14)	8 years
Samson	Chapters 13–16	Dan	Philistines	40 years (13:1)	20 years (15:20; 16:31)	60 years

Israel's sin led to oppression by foreign nations. Foreigners oppressed the Israelites, because they disobeyed God. They did not live as redeemed-foreigners. They lived as pagans among pagans, as non-redeemed foreigners. It is only after God chooses a Moabite foreigner that things changed significantly for God's people.

Enter Ruth.

Ruth The Foreigner Kingmaker

The book of Judges ends in hopelessness. Further, hopelessness introduces the narrative of the book of Ruth. The book begins by setting the immediate context in which the next main character of the redemptive narrative story—Ruth—found herself. Next, we are introduced to another foreigner. Abimelech, who attempted to escape famine with his family, sojourned (*guwr*) to the land of Moab with his wife and sons. Unfortunately, his fate and that of his sons ended in death. While in the land, his sons took Moabite wives. Orpah and Ruth, alongside Naomi (Abimelech's wife), alone survived.

In ancient times women depended on their status as wives to survive. What were these three women to do? They were now homeless, husbandless, and landless. They were bound for certain calamity. After much suffering Naomi urged her daughters-in-law to return to their homeland and abandon her. Though Orpah left to return to her family, Ruth clung to Naomi. The reason? Well, let's hear it from Ruth herself,

> But Ruth said, "Do not urge me to leave you or to return from following you. For where you go I will go, and where you lodge I will lodge. Your people shall be my people, and your God my God. Where you die I will die, and there I will be buried. May the Lord do so to me and more also if anything but death parts me from you" (Ruth 1:16–17).

Ruth's decision to follow Naomi's God changed everything. Though she was a Moabite by birth, she was an Israelite by faith. She was a redeemed-foreigner.

Upon returning to Bethlehem with Naomi, Ruth immediately became a foreigner. Up to that point in her life she did not know what it meant to be one. But from then on she began being referred to as "Ruth the Moabite" (Ruth 2:2; 6; 21; 4:5; 10). This foreigner––weak, fragile, hungry, widowed, and homeless–– would eventually be restored. By God's providence Ruth met Boaz, who was a family "kinsman redeemer." In other words, he was someone able to properly claim Ruth as his wife.

Ruth the Moabite married Boaz the Israelite from the tribe of Judah. At the end of the book's narrative, she is no longer referred to as "Ruth the Moabite." She is simply Ruth. Ruth 4:13 records, "So Boaz took Ruth, and she became his wife. And he went into her, and the Lord gave her conception, and she bore a son." Ruth became a precursor for the coming of the Messiah (Ruth 4:17–22).

Ruth the foreigner became the conduit from which God would accomplish his goal to bring about the "obedience of the nations." Back in Genesis 49, Jacob prophesied the following: 1) Judah's brother's would praise him, 2) he would rule over his enemies while his father's sons would pay him homage, 3) he would be like a lion's cub and like a lion who crouches and a lioness who no one dares to challenge, 4) he would be like a king who rules with a scepter in his hands while the nations submit to his authority. Judah was to hold a special place in God's redemptive history. Judah's rule can be traced through David, Ruth's grandson.

It is Ruth's grandson, David, who became the recipient of a new covenant that would forever change the fate of God's people and of all humankind.

CHAPTER FOUR

Of Kings and Foreigners

"The problem with many modern Christians is that they feel too much at home in the world" – A W. Tozer

G uess what? Foreigners owe allegiance to their home country. As a young child I studied the history, structure, and norms of Brazilian society. I remember lining up as a young man in a single file line to sing the Brazilian national anthem. Our teachers––as is done in nations across the globe––wanted to instill in us a sense of belonging and patriotism. However, these practices faded over time. We were only required to sing the national anthem until eighth grade.

When I came to America, I was surprised by the level of patriotism Americans displayed. Not only was there a pledge of allegiance to the flag of the United States, but every ball game began with the playing of the national anthem. From secondary schools to professional sports patriotism was in full display. After I became a citizen of the United States, I too pledged allegiance to the flag of the United States. And every time the United States national anthem is sung, I feel great pride.

There is something honorable about pledging allegiance to the ideals of your nation. However, as redeemed-foreigners our greatest allegiance belongs to God and his Kingdom and not to America as a nation. Politics, patriotism, national pride, and cultural values are secondary to our allegiance to our Lord. We can easily be deceived into thinking this world is our home. When this happens, the consequences can be devastating to our witness for Jesus.

The nation of Israel was lured into pledging allegiance to human institutions and man-made idols, rather than to God. Israel had been redeemed from slavery in Egypt. God dwelt among them in the wilderness, specifically in the tabernacle. God protected them, saved them from starvation, famine, and disease. He led them through the desert with great care, day and night. Exodus 13:21 records, "And the LORD went before them by day in a pillar of cloud to *lead them along the way*, and by night in a pillar of fire to give them light, that they might travel by day and by night." As their leader, he provided for all their needs. In Deuteronomy 29:5, God reminded his people, "I have led you forty years in the wilderness; your clothes have not worn out on you, and your sandals have not worn off your feet." So, one may wonder, what better leader could there be for Israel than God himself?

The refusal of Israel's leaders to serve the Lord with all their heart, soul, and might, permeates the narratives of the Old Testament. God's people were oppressed by foreign nations, they were subjugated because of their rebellion, and often refused to worship God for other foreign entities. Their disobedience and ingratitude are clearly seen in 1 and 2 Samuel. In fact, 1 Samuel begins by underscoring how the priests of the nation had become wicked and weak. They had turned the temple, as many would in future times, into a wicked commercial center rather than a place of worship.

But God who is rich in mercy continued to pursue his people with great compassion. He provided for them one final judge before he picked Israel's first king. His name was Samuel, which in Hebrew means "God heard."

Samuel had been dedicated to God by his mother, Hannah. He replaced Eli and his worthless sons. Samuel became Israel's last judge before the Israeli monarchy was established. Prior to Samuel's ascension, Eli's sons Hophni and Phinehas (more like "numbnuts" number 1 and "numbnuts" number 2), decided it was a great idea to take the ark of the covenant into battle against the Philistines. After a fierce battle, the ark of the covenant wound up in the hands of a foreign nation for the first time ever in their history. After a series of events, the ark was sent back to the Israelites.

Samuel ruled as a judge following such tragic events. During his time as a judge no foreign nation came against Israel. The Philistines were subdued. They did not enter the territory of Israel. Because the Lord was with Samuel the Philistines no longer were a problem for the Israelites. Further, the cities they had previously conquered were restored and there was peace between Israel and the Amorites (1 Samuel 7:13–14).

Samuel ruled well through his latter earthly years, but not at home. His sons did not turn out to be suitable leaders. His sons became like Eli's sons (1 Samuel 8:3). This prompted the elders of Israel to ask Samuel for a new leader. But not just any leader. The Israelites wanted a king. They wanted Samuel to appoint a king to rule over Israel "like all the nations." They were not content with having God ruling over them, they wanted an earthly representative (1 Samuel 8:5–6). Note that the Israelites desired to be like all the other nations because perhaps they thought the other nations had it right. This was their greatest weakness. They had God as their ruler. Again, what better ruler is there than God himself?

Samuel was "displeased" with their request. Maybe because they called him "old" (nobody likes being called "old man")? Maybe because he wished his sons would rule? It is hard to know. However, God answered the elders' request in the affirmative while at the same time issuing a warning. Samuel felt rejected. However, he was not the only one being rejected, the people were rejecting God as their king (1 Samuel 8:7).

Throughout Scripture God's rule is challenged, rejected, and at times despised. The theme of his kingdom rule is found throughout. However, mankind often rejected (and still does) his dominion. God is the ultimate ruler, but the breaking of the first and second commandments are the ongoing theme of both the Israelites and the other foreign nations. 1 Samuel 8 shows that the elders' obstinance and rejection of God did not waver. Are you surprised? Even after being warned of the consequences of such inquiry, they still wanted to be like the other foreign nations (1 Samuel 8:19–20).

Enter Saul.

God chose Saul from the tribe of Benjamin to become Israel's first monarch. Though he was called handsome, his appearance did not turn into winsome leadership. Saul began well. After he was anointed, God supernaturally gives him his Spirit to defeat their foreign neighbors the Ammonites (1 Samuel 11). But Saul tried to take matters into his own hands. He sinned against God in disobedience. Then, he lied to Samuel when confronted. Soon the Philistines came after Saul and his kingdom.

Saul turned out to be a terrible ruler. At one point, after Samuel's death, he consulted a witch from Endor, a foreign Canaanite medium, to inquire about a battle he was to face against the Philistines. His doom was forthcoming. Saul was defeated, fled from the hands of the foreign Philistines, and committed suicide.

Enter David.

David The Foreigner

David's story intersected with Saul's life and reign. After God rejected Saul's kingship (1 Samuel 15:34–35), he quickly moved to anoint a new king. God's Spirit came upon David and immediately departed from Saul. David, by God's providence, wound up in Saul's court and he was tasked to console Saul. In the midst of Saul's reign, the foreign Philistines came against the Israelites. This time they brought out the big guns. Goliath, a giant warrior, together with an army of the Philistines came into the Valley of Elah (a territory of Israel) to torment and mock God and his people.

David was only a young shepherd when he faced Goliath, but he was fierce. His anger toward Goliath was fueled by his passion for God, the God of Israel. In fact, the Bible showcases David's bravery and godly courage, as seen in his words to Goliath. The giant tried to intimate David with his ginormous spear and javelin. But David declared, "I come to you in the name of the Lord of hosts, the God of the armies of Israel." David not only invoked God's name, but he called out Goliath's blasphemous attitude. He knew the Lord would deliver the giant warrior into his hands. He fought him filled with faith and courage. With powerful language, he also told Goliath he would cut off his head, a small detail I am pretty sure most Sunday School teachers leave out of the story. And why did David fight Goliath? Not for personal gain. Not for bragging rights. Not to receive accolades and the king's prize. He fought him so "that all the earth may know that there is a God in Israel," that everyone present on that day would know the Lord alone saves, and that he is the one who wins battles! (1 Samuel 17:45–47).

David won the battle. He killed the taunting giant foreigner. As David's fame increased, so did Saul's jealousy. Saul began to persecute David and tried to kill him several times. David fled for his life. At first David fled to a few places in Israel. But Saul's minions kept pursuing him. Eventually, David fled to Gath of the Philistines (1 Samuel 21:10). David became a foreigner.

David became a sojourner among the Moabites (1 Samuel 22:3) and the Philistines (1 Samuel 27:3). After the death of Saul and Jonathan, David was anointed king of Judah (2 Samuel 2). Soon after he was anointed king over all of Israel (2 Samuel 5). It was during his early monarchical years that God established the Messianic Davidic covenant with David.

David inquired of the prophet Nathan to build a house of worship for the Lord. Keep in mind that up to this point God's tabernacle was completely gone. There was no local central place of worship for God's people in the land of Israel. In fact, God reminded David, "I have not lived in a house since the day I brought up the people of Israel from Egypt to this day, but I have been moving about in a tent for my dwelling" (2 Samuel 7:2). Therefore, David wanted to build a temple where God could dwell in their midst once again. God replied to David with a much greater plan. A new covenant was established. The last covenant God had established with his people dated back to Moses.

God told David of his intentions (2 Samuel 7:10–16). First, he would appoint a dwelling place for Israel in order to plant them somewhere they would not be disturbed by other peoples. Second, God desired to give his people rest from their enemies. Third, he told David he would make him a house. David wanted to build God a house, but instead God decided he would build one for him instead. Fourth, this house figuratively referred to David's seed (offspring) whose kingdom would be established by God himself. Fifth, David's house would bear God's own name. What a privilege, right? It was through this name that God would establish an eternal kingdom. Finally, the throne of David's seed would become an everlasting kingdom.

David's plans were more earthly-minded, God's plans were eternal. David wanted to establish an earthly dwelling for God, but God wanted to establish a heavenly dwelling for his people through the work of his Messiah. Like Abraham, God would make David's name great. He would use his offspring, or "seed." The use of the word "seed" evokes the promises of God to Abraham and his seed in Genesis. God chose David's descendant to become Israel's ultimate king. His eternal kingdom would fulfill the Abrahamic covenant through whom "all the nations of the earth would be blessed" (Genesis 12:3b).

The nations soon felt God's hand and favor was over David and Israel. In 2 Samuel 8, David subdued the many foreign nations who often stood against God's people. During this lifetime David subdued the nations of Edom, Moab, the Ammonites, the

Philistines, Amalek, and took from the spoil of Hadadezer the son of Rehob, king of Zobah. He conquered and subdued them taking their gold and silver. David also defeated the Syrians (2 Samuel 10). Peace came over the land of Israel as promised by God (2 Samuel 7:11). But this peace was short-lived.

In 2 Samuel 11, David gravely sinned against God. The consequences were disastrous. Hamilton writes, "David's sin with Bathsheba is the nation's first step in the direction of exile, and his transgression sets the trajectory of trespass that leads straight to Babylon."[22] Not only did he lose his son born of adultery, but his family dismantled. His son Absalom killed his half-brother Amnon. Fleeing for his life, Absalom fled to live among the Gershurites, an independent Aramean kingdom (2 Samuel 13:34–39). Absalom became a foreigner.

Absalom is described as a very handsome young man (2 Samuel 14:25). His description is similar to the description given to David when he was a young man soon to be chosen and anointed to become Israel's king (1 Samuel 16:12). It was Absalom's handsomely appearance that likely earned him a following. The Bible tells us Absalom "stole the hearts" of the people of Israel (2 Samuel 15:6). His influence eventually led to a revolt. Absalom managed to overpower his father by raising his own army against him.

David's saga with Absalom turned the land of Israel into disarray. While Absalom established his rule from Jerusalem, David fled for his life. Later Absalom died and David returned to rule the nation of Israel in Judah. It was only during the reign of Solomon that Israel prospered beyond measure. Jonathan Akin writes, "Through the wise reigns of David and Solomon, the Lord was re-establishing human dominion and providing a picture of the coming Messianic Kingdom that will stretch from sea to sea and include all the peoples of the earth (Psalm 72)."[23]

Solomon The Lover Of Foreigners

Solomon's reign was established in the midst of conflict. However, he succeeded David to the throne of Israel. Solomon became an important player in the history of God's redemption. He finished the construction of the temple in Jerusalem. He brought peace to Israel during his reign. Solomon was given the task to build an Eden-like temple for God's dwelling. Graeme Goldsworthy writes, "The thematic progression, then, is Eden, Promised Land (denied in Egypt, then achieved), the land focused on the tabernacle and then on the temple in Jerusalem. Attaching to the temple is the demonstration of God's presence often described as his glory."[24] Furthermore, Hamilton points out, "The description of the garden of Eden is echoed in the descriptions of the tabernacle and the temple ... a cosmic temple, a holy dwelling place of God. "[25]

God's presence among his people rested upon the temple. It also rested over Solomon and manifested itself in his divinely given wisdom. In Scripture, his wisdom and insights are recorded in the books of Proverbs and Ecclesiastes. Upon ascending to the throne of Israel, God appeared to Solomon in a dream. In genie-like fashion God told Solomon to ask anything he desired. Surprisingly, instead of asking for riches, fame, and power, Solomon simply asked the Lord for wisdom:

> And Solomon said, "You have shown great and steadfast love to your servant David my father, because he walked before you in faithfulness, in righteousness, and in up-

rightness of heart toward you. And you have kept for him this great and steadfast love and have given him a son to sit on his throne this day. And now, O Lord my God, you have made your servant king in place of David my father, although I am but a little child. I do not know how to go out or come in. And your servant is in the midst of your people whom you have chosen, a great people, too many to be numbered or counted for multitude. Give your servant therefore an understanding mind to govern your people, that I may discern between good and evil, for who is able to govern this your great people?" (1 Kings 3:6–9).

The Lord was pleased with his request. The Lord told Solomon he would grant his request:

> *Behold, I give you a wise and discerning mind,* so that none like you has been before you and none like you shall arise after you. *I give you also what you have not asked, both riches and honor, so that no other king shall compare with you, all your days* (1 Kings 3:12–13).

Solomon became the wisest man to walk the earth (1 Kings 4:29–31). He also ruled over all the major foreign powers of his day (1 Kings 4:20–24). Solomon's renown became known among the nations: "And people of all nations came to hear the wisdom of Solomon, and from all the kings of the earth, who had heard of his wisdom" (1 Kings 4:34). Gentile nations flocked to hear about his wisdom. Queen Sheba's visit is an example of how foreigners viewed Solomon. She visited Solomon because his wisdom's fame was widespread.

Solomon's kingdom was inclusive. He understood his role as a unifier of nations. In 1 Kings 8, Solomon's prayer mentions the foreigner. He pleads before God to answer the prayer of any believing foreigner. He asked God to answer the foreigner's prayer when he approached God's temple, asking God to hear his prayer from his heavenly dwelling place. The reason? So that when a foreigner called to the Lord "all the peoples of the earth" would know God's name and fear Him. Though Solomon's plea is directed toward foreigner believers, the emphasis of the prayer is on God's name (1 Kings 8:41–43).

God's promise to Abraham was that his descendants would bless all the nations of the earth. From the beginning God wanted to redeem all foreigners into heavenly-dwellers. The reign of Solomon became a small glimpse of God's desire for the nations to be drawn to worship him forever.

Solomon seemed to be fulfilling the Abrahamic promise. As people came from all nations to hear of his wisdom, one can only wonder why Israel's kingdom did not remain strong for long. Though Solomon accomplished the building of the temple, peace in the land, and great prosperity, he squandered his kingdom by leading it into a chaotic direction.

Among foreigners, Solomon was the wisest and most prosperous, excelling above all other earthly rulers (1 Kings 10:23). But Solomon, like every other human being that has walked the earth, was not fully satisfied by his power, fame, and riches. He turned away from the God of his father David. The problem? He loved foreign women.

Solomon had 700 wives and 300 concubines (1 Kings 11:3). For most of his life he avoided their pagan worship.[26] But his heart turned. 1 Kings 11:4 records how Solomon turned away to false gods because of the influence of his wives in his old age. Akin points out, "The reign of Solomon does not last, however, because Solomon loves and marries 'foreign' women who turn his heart away from the Lord to idols" (1 Kings 11:1ff.). By taking foreign wives, Solomon violated the kingly law of Deuteronomy 17, bringing judgment upon himself and his house."[27] When other people and things succeed in replacing our worship of God the consequences are disastrous. Not only that, but the consequences of such rebellion are also often practical. Because of Solomon's rebellion God sent foreign kings and nations against him. Furthermore, his kingdom began to crumble from within.

Kings And Foreigners

Israel would never again see such splendor as in the days of king Solomon. Soon after his demise, Jeroboam, one of his servants, rebelled against him. Jeroboam, an Israelite, became a foreigner in the land of Egypt after escaping Solomon's persecution (1 Kings 11:40). But this Israelite foreigner would still be one of the main catalysts for the split of Israel's monarchy. Though Solomon's son Rehoboam was appointed king over Israel his dynasty was dismantled. Israel's short-lived unity ended after the three kings Saul, David, and Solomon.

The author of Kings points out that there was continual warfare between Rehoboam and Jeroboam. Further, other foreigners, like Shishak King of Egypt came against Rehoboam. Rehoboam's downfall is highlighted by the fact he was the son of one of Solomon's foreign wives. The author makes it a point to write: "His mother's name was Naamah; she was an Ammonite" (1 Kings 14:21 and 31).

The Israelites were divided into the kingdom of Israel to the north under Jeroboam, and the kingdom of Judah to the south led by Rehoboam. The majority of Israel and Judah's subsequent kings failed to serve the Lord. It is after this time that God's people began to long once again for a king like David. Though failure followed, hopes for the promised Messianic king did not. Their hopes pointed back to the Davidic covenant.

Unfortunately, many wicked kings rose to power. King Ahab became the most wicked king. His wickedness was well documented. He not only did more evil than all those who preceded him, he worshiped Baal, and built an altar to this false god while also making an Asherah. Scripture says, "And Ahab made an Asherah. Ahab did more to provoke the Lord, the God of Israel, to anger than all the kings of Israel who were before him" (1 Kings 16:33).

Ahab married a foreigner named Jezebel. Jezebel was a Baal worshipper. She was a wicked woman. Ahab, like Solomon, let his foreigner wife turn his worship from the true God to the foreign god Baal. Eventually, Ahab died at the hands of foreigners. The Syrians killed him in battle.

The kingdoms of Israel and Judah seemed hopeless. Destruction, chaos, war, famine, and much more ensued in the land. The glimpses of hope were small as only a few remained faithful to God. Prophets arose from among the people to confront the evils of the land. The first of them was Elijah, who was taken up to heaven miraculously (2 Kings 2). His successor, Elisha, shows how the hope for the nation of Israel and Gentile foreigners intertwined. Elisha not only provided oil for a Shunammite woman whose husband died, but he also raised her foreigner son from death to life (2 Kings 4). Further, he healed a foreign Syrian army commander who had been struck with leprosy. Elijah and Elisha became types of Christ.

In the years to come the Israelites would experience oppression. Eventually both the northern kingdom and the southern kingdom were conquered. God's people were exiled in Assyria and Babylon. The fall of Israel happened during the reign of Hoshea. God's people became foreigners in Assyria as God had the Assyrians take them away into captivity (2 Kings 17:6).

Not since Israel's captivity in Egypt had God's people been exiled from the Promised Land. They had forsaken the Lord and turned away to false gods who were in fact not gods at all (2 Kings 17:7–12).

The Promised Land, which once belonged to Israel, was resettled with foreigners from distant lands. 2 Kings 17:24 records, "And the king of Assyria brought people from Babylon, Cuthah, Avva, Hamath, and Sepharvaim, and placed them in the cities of Samaria instead of the people of Israel. And they took possession of Samaria and lived in its cities." The exile happened as a result of years of bad leadership and nationwide rebellion against God. Especially from Israel's kings.

Only two kings stood out from among their peers. First, Hezekiah did what was right in God's eyes (2 Kings 18:3). His deeds were indeed praiseworthy, but not enough. After he tried to appease the Babylonians, God used the prophet Isaiah to tell him eventually God's people would be carried to Babylon as foreign captives (2 Kings 20:12–21).

Second, Josiah brought great reform to the land of Israel after years of rebellion and neglect of worship. He restored the Passover celebration, put away mediums, necromancers, the household gods and idols and all other abominations from the land of Judah and in Jerusalem (2 Kings 23:24). He was the odd exception. The Bible tells us, "Before him there was no king like him, who turned to the Lord with all his heart and with all his soul and with all his might, according to all the Law of Moses, nor did any like him arise after him" (2 Kings 23:25).

However, Josiah's reform and short-lived revival did not prevent the exile of God's people. God's wrath was still kindled against his people. He justly punished them. God's wrath was not necessarily aimed at king Josiah as much as it was Manasseh. The Israelites were exile-bound. The Lord declared, "I will remove Judah also out of my sight, as I have removed Israel, and I will cast off this city that I have chosen, Jerusalem, and the house of which I said, My name shall be there" (2 Kings 23:27).

Manasseh was a wicked king. He is described as being worse than the foreigners who conquered God's people (2 Kings 21:9). God's judgment rained down on his people because of their wickedness. Though he warned them through the word of the prophets, their obstinance remained. This was the beginning of the Jewish Diaspora.

This helpful progression may help us track the biblical story plotline up to this point:

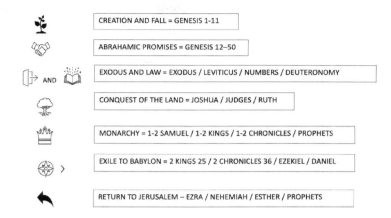

CREATION AND FALL = GENESIS 1-11

ABRAHAMIC PROMISES = GENESIS 12–50

EXODUS AND LAW = EXODUS / LEVITICUS / NUMBERS / DEUTERONOMY

CONQUEST OF THE LAND = JOSHUA / JUDGES / RUTH

MONARCHY = 1-2 SAMUEL / 1-2 KINGS / 1-2 CHRONICLES / PROPHETS

EXILE TO BABYLON = 2 KINGS 25 / 2 CHRONICLES 36 / EZEKIEL / DANIEL

RETURN TO JERUSALEM – EZRA / NEHEMIAH / ESTHER / PROPHETS

Do not forget, the ultimate goal of God for humankind is to take us from foreigners to redeemed-foreigners, and from redeemed-foreigners to future eternal heavenly-citizens.

CHAPTER FIVE

Prophets, Foreign Nations, and Exile

This world is not my home, I'm just a passing through
My treasures are laid up somewhere beyond the blue The
angels beckon me from heaven's open door. And I can't feel
at home in this world anymore – Albert E. Brumley

G uess what? All foreigners are invited to enter the kingdom of God. God planned to save people for himself
from all peoples on earth. Jews and Gentiles are welcomed in God's kingdom. But the privilege of participation
in God's kingdom is only reserved for those who submit to
him by faith. Jews thought God's kingdom belonged to them
simply because God chose them as a nation. However, God's
purpose was to save both Jewish and Gentile believers. Paul declared that the gospel is for both Jewish and Gentile believers
(Romans 1:16–17).

The Israelites were in constant contact with foreigners.
Once in the Promised Land they lived among foreign peoples
like the Canaanites and the Philistines. The Philistines, for instance, dwelt in villages within the Promised Land. Further,
Transjordanian peoples like the Ammonites, Moabites, and
Edomites shared the land with them. God knew this was going
to be the case. Further, he also predicted his people's rebellion

back in Deuteronomy 29 and 30.

In Deuteronomy 29, God spoke of future generations who would rebel against him and be punished. He told them the nations would wonder why he would scatter them in the future, "All the nations will ask: 'Why has the Lord done this to this land? Why this fierce, burning anger?'" (Deuteronomy 29:24). If the Israelites were God's chosen people, why would they be sent to exile, suffer harm, and be judged so severely? The answer is simple: rebellion. They behaved like non-redeemed foreigners.

This behavior was nothing new. The Israelites had a history of rebellion and obstinacy. Speaking of a future time Moses once said,

> Then people will say, "It is because they abandoned the covenant of the Lord, the God of their fathers, which he made with them when he brought them out of the land of Egypt and went and served other gods and worshiped them" (Deuteronomy 29:25–26).

God's plan from the beginning was for the Israelites to be a "light unto the nations." The prophet Isaiah alludes to this reality, "It is too light a thing that you should be my servant to raise up the tribes of Jacob and to bring back the preserved of Israel; I will make you as a light for the nations, that my salvation may reach to the end of the earth" (Isaiah 49:6). The chosen nation of Israel was meant to bring the salvation of all peoples. But instead, their sin and rebellion led them into exile. Their obstinance and prone-to-idolatry attitude was punished by God as he judged their sin. After the Israeli monarchy, they were sent into exile until their rebellion was atoned for and their hearts turned back to God.

Small rays of light were seen during the time of the exile. Four people stand out in the Biblical narrative: Daniel, Esther, Ezra, and Nehemiah. But first, let's focus on Israel's prophets. Rather than remaining pure, Israel defiled itself by following the ways of other foreign nations. Israel's monarchy was marred with unfortunate and painful events. Sexual immorality, necromancy, child sacrifices, cult prostitution, and other evil acts were not only permitted, but encouraged by Israel's kings. It is in the midst of such disgusting reality that God sent his prophets.

The Hebrew word for prophet is *nabi*. The Gesenius Hebrew-Chaldee Lexicon describes a "prophet" as one "who had actuated by a divine afflatus [inspiration], or spirit, either rebuked the conduct of kings and nations, or predicted future events (i.e., Deuteronomy 13:2; Judges 6:8; 1 Samuel 9:9; 1 Kings 22:7; 2 Kings 3:11)."[28] They acted as emissaries. They were heralds of good news and messengers of calamity and judgment.

In ancient times the prophets spoke on behalf of God, as if God himself was speaking. Phrases such as "Thus, says the Lord God of Israel" (2 Kings 22:15–17), "Thus says the Lord God" (Ezekiel 38:170), and "As I live declares the Lord" (Ezekiel 17:16), are a few examples. Sadly, because evil ran rampant amid God's people, the prophets issued more words of warning and calamity than not, sometimes in very descriptive ways (i.e., Isaiah 5).

God warned his people that they would wind up in exile. Simply read the major and minor prophets of the Old Testament, for example. He warned them of captivity to foreign nations. God chose two nations to take his people into captivity for their rebellion, Assyria and Babylon. The prophecies in the monarchical time were directed toward both Judah and Israel.

But God also prophesied against the pagan nations he selected to punish his people. Only three of the prophets (Haggai, Zechariah, and Malachi) of this period in Israel's history were post-exilic.

BIBLICAL PROPHETS

Pre-exilic Prophets - Before the Captivity of Northern Kingdom (Israel)

Jonah	Nineveh (Assyria)	King Jeroboam II
Hosea	Prophesied to Israel	Kings: Jeroboam II, Zechariah, Shallum, Menahem, Pekaniah, Pekah, Hoshea
Amos	Prophesied to Israel	King Jeroboam II

Pre-exilic Prophets - Before the Captivity of Southern Kingdom (Judah)

Nahum	Prophesied to Nineveh (Assyria)	Kings: Manasseh, Amon, Josiah
Obadiah	Prophesied to Edom	King Zedekiah
Isaiah	Prophesied to Judah	Kings: Uzziah, Jotham, Ahaz, Hezekiah, Manasseh
Jeremiah/Lamentations	Prophesied to Judah	Kings: Josiah, Jehoahaz, Jehoiakim, Jeholachin, Zedekiah
Joel	Prophesied to Judah	King Joash
Micah	Prophesied to Judah	Kings Jotham, Ahaz, Hezekiah, Manasseh
Habakkuk	Prophesied to Judah	Kings Jehoiakim, Jeholachin
Zephaniah	Prophesied to Judah	Amon, Josiah

Prophets – During Southern Kingdom Captivity (Babylon)

Ezekiel	Prophesied to Judah in Exile	Kings Jehoiakim, Hezekiah
Daniel	Prophesied to Judah in Exile	Kings Jehoiakim, Jeholachin, Zedekiah

Post-exilic Prophets – After the Captivity of Southern Kingdom (Judah)

Haggai	Prophesied to the Returned Remnant of Judah	Governor Zerubbabel
Zechariah	Prophesied to the Returned Remnant of Judah	Governor Zerubbabel
Malachi	Prophesied to the Returned Remnant of Judah	Governor Nehemiah

The prophets found themselves in three main contexts: pre-exile, in-exile, and post-exile. Further, they prophesied about future exile and punishment for the kingdoms of Israel and Judah. God's people sinned gravely against him. Just as Adam was exiled from Eden, Israel was exiled from the Promised Land. A full examination of each of these prophets is beyond the scope of my work. However, the prophet Isaiah, the first of the Major prophets, is representative of what we see throughout the prophets.

Isaiah And The Nations

Isaiah is the most prominent of all the Old Testament prophetic books. Isaiah is a pinnacle prophet. Isaiah, some have noted, is like a miniature Bible. There is a twofold message of condemnation (1–39) and consolation/hope (40–66) that permeates the book. Isaiah analyzes the sins of Judah and pronounces God's judgment on the nation. Judgment, however, was also applied against foreign nations.

Judgment was pronounced against the following nations: Babylon (13:1–14:23), Assyria (14:24–27), the Philistines (14:28–32), Moab (15–16), Syria and Israel (17), Ethiopia (18), Egypt (19), Egypt and Cush (20), Babylon (21:1–10), Edom (21:11–12), Arabia (21:13–17), Jerusalem (22), Tyre (23). Isaiah's prophetic ministry spanned the reigns of four kings of Judah and covered a period of at least 40 years. Though much of the book contains words of condemnation, hope was always on the horizon:

> They lift up their voices; they sing for joy; over the majesty of the LORD, they shout from the west. Therefore, in
>
> the east give glory to the LORD; in the coastlands of the sea, give glory to the name of the LORD, the God of Israel (Isaiah 24:14–15).

The salvation offered to Israel is also offered to foreigners from pagan nations who repent. The God of Israel invited the nations to worship him.

The basic theme of the book is found in Isaiah's name which means "salvation is of the Lord". The word "salvation" appears twenty-six times in Isaiah but only seven times in all the other prophets combined. Interestingly enough, the Neviim (the second section of the TANAK) begins with Joshua, and the next major section begins with Isaiah (Major prophets), and the final part with Hosea (The Twelve Minor prophets). The name of each of these prophets means "Salvation," or "God saves", or "Salvation is of the Lord." The root of their name is the same root for the name "Jesus." Conclusion? The prophets of the Old Testament foreshadowed the ultimate prophet, Jesus Christ.

In Isaiah, the Messiah is portrayed as one who will draw all peoples to himself (Isaiah 52:13; Philippians 2:9–10). One of the main thrusts of the book of Isaiah is found at the very beginning. Isaiah 2:2-3:

> It shall come to pass in the latter days
> that the **mountain** of the house of the LORD
> shall be established as the highest of the mountains,
> and shall be lifted up above the hills;
> *and all the **nations** shall flow to it,*
> *and many **peoples** shall come,* and say:
> "Come, let us go up to the **mountain** of the LORD,
> to the house of the God of Jacob,
> that he may teach us his ways
> and that we may walk in his paths."
> For out of **Zion** shall go forth the law,
> and the word of the LORD from **Jerusalem**.

The Mountain

In the beginning after God created the heavens and the earth, he placed Adam and Eve in the garden of Eden. The garden is described as a lush and beautiful place. It was full of trees that were pleasing to look at and delicious for food (Genesis 2:9). Four rivers ran through the garden adorning its beauty and highlighting its richness (Genesis 2:10–14). The Creator placed Adam and Eve in paradise, and he fellowshipped with them (Genesis 3:8).

A simple reading of Genesis 3:6 reveals that Adam and Eve were not content with all the other trees, though they were pleasing to the eyes. Rather, they disobeyed God's command and ate from the tree of the knowledge of good and evil that was placed in the middle of the garden (Genesis 2:16–17). Their "eyes" were deceived:

> When the woman *saw* that the fruit of the tree was good for food and *pleasing to the eye*, and also desirable for gaining wisdom, she took some and ate it. She also gave some to her husband, who was with her, and he ate it (Genesis 3:6).

Their mistake is known as the Fall of mankind. As mentioned in the first chapter of the book, Adam and Eve were exiled from the garden and lost fellowship with God. This consequential event is the reason there is so much chaos in our world. But even though Adam and Eve rebelled against God and deserved to die, God, who is rich in mercy, crafted a plan to restore humankind's broken relationship with him.

The progression of God's plan is highlighted throughout

the Old Testament, and most vividly in Isaiah. Hamilton writes, "Through the judgment of the exile, the shoot will sprout from that holy seed to bring salvation (cf. 11:1), Jerusalem will be exalted (2:1–5), and the glory of God will cover Mount Zion (4:5)."[29] The grand narrative of Scripture reveals God's intention to dwell among humans created in the *imago Dei* remains the same. The two most vivid examples are the wilderness Tabernacle and the Jerusalem Temple. Though God used the nation of Israel to fulfill his plans through the Messiah, his ultimate goal is for all to be saved (i.e., 1 Timothy 2:4; 2 Peter 3:9). He wants to redeem mankind (who became foreigners after the Fall) in order to make them heavenly citizens.

The mountain motif is found in the Torah, the Prophets, and the Writings. After God had delivered the Israelites from Egypt, he took them into the wilderness. A massive caravan of foreigners eventually found themselves at the foot of Mount Sinai. God's glory came over Mount Sinai, and prior to God's descent he tells Moses,

> Go to the people and consecrate them today and tomorrow, and let them wash their garments and be ready for the third day. For on the third day the Lord will come down on Mount Sinai in the sight of all the people. And you shall set limits for the people all around, saying, "Take care not to go up into the mountain or touch the edge of it. Whoever touches the mountain shall be put to death" (Exodus 19:10–12).

No one was allowed on the Lord's mountain at this point. DeYoung and Gilbert write, "God may have chosen them and rescued them, but their sin remains and mankind's exile from Eden is still in effect."[30] The mountain motif in Sinai points to the mountain motif in Zion. Eventually, all people groups on earth will gather there, on God's holy mountain, to worship him.

The Old Testament reveals the progression from garden to mountain to city. The Lord in the end picked Jerusalem as a central place for worship. Jerusalem is an elevated place, geographically speaking. It is literally on top of a mountain. Hence why Isaiah 2:2 says, "the *mountain* of the house of the LORD, shall be established as the highest of the mountains." He is not talking about mount Everest here. Rather, he is referring to Mount Zion. It is on this mountain that the nations will flock to worship God. This same reality is also described by the prophet Micah: "Many nations will come, and say, 'Come, let us go up to the *mountain* of the LORD, to the house of the God of Jacob, that he may teach us his ways and that we may walk in his paths'" (Micah 4:1–3a).

During the reign of Solomon, Zion was the place where the temple was placed. In 1 Kings 8, Solomon and the elders of Jerusalem bring the ark of the covenant of the Lord to Zion, the city of David, and after the temple is dedicated by the priests "the glory of Lord filled his temple" (1 Kings 8:10). If you follow the narrative of the Old Testament, the glory of God did not remain in the temple for very long. His presence was withdrawn.

The mountain motif runs throughout Scripture. First, Moses received the law at Mount Sinai. Second, mountain Zion became the place where the people of God worship him. This place, located in Jerusalem, became a precursor of a later time when all peoples will worship God on the heavenly city of Jerusalem on Mount Zion. In the New Testament, many of Jesus' settings took place on mountains: Jesus' temptation (Matthew 4:8) the Sermon on the Mount (Matthew 5:1–12), a number of healings (Matthew 15:29-31), the event at the Mount of Transfiguration (Matthew 17:1), Jesus' final discourse (Matthew 24:3), and the commissioning of the 12 apostles (Matthew 28:16-20). But the ultimate place where all peoples will gather is Mount Zion.

Illustration by Sarah Lynn Miller
Isaiah 2:3 – "The Gathering of the Nations"

This illustration is a reminder of the coming Messiah who will draw all peoples to himself.
In Isaiah 2:3 it is written that the "many people" will gather up and go to the mountain of
Zion - to the temple of "the God of Jacob" where they will be taught his ways and given the
command to go out from Zion, taking with them the word of the LORD from Jerusalem.
Shown in the sketch are "the many people" coming to the mountain to worship God

The Nations

Isaiah, inspired by the Holy Spirit, envisioned a day when "nations" and "peoples" would be drawn to the mountain of the Lord to worship. God desires for all nations to come to him. The Hebrew word for "nations" is *goyim*. In the Old Testament this word is used in reference to established nations, to heathens, or Gentiles. Even in modern times the word *goy* is used in reference to non-Jews.

Reference to the nations appears throughout the prophets (i.e., Isaiah 10:7; Jeremiah 1:5; Ezekiel 2:3; Daniel 8:22; Hosea 8:10; Joel 2:17; Amos 6:1; Obadiah 1:1; Micah 4:2; Nahum 3:5; Habakkuk 1:17; Zephaniah 3:6; Haggai 2:7; Zechariah 2:8; Malachi 3:12). The picture of Isaiah 2 involves the coming of the Lord to rule, judge, over the nations. Furthermore, the Messianic description of the "son" in Isaiah 9 reveals the coming of a ruling Messiah.

Isaiah describes him, saying, "the government shall be upon his shoulder." And these beautiful words are uttered:

> Of the increase of his government and of peace
> there will be no end,
> on the throne of David and over his kingdom,
> to establish it and to uphold it
> with justice and with righteousness
> from this time forth and forevermore.
> The zeal of the LORD of hosts will do this (Isaiah 9:7)

Christ the Savior would rule one day, and all the nations of the earth would be drawn to worship him. Today, the nations are being gathered to him. The task of missions is to accomplish

God's mission. His mission includes the ingathering of all re-deemed-foreigners to himself to live as heavenly dwellers with him forever.

Isaiah's focus is on the Messiah, the Christ. Isaiah 53 is per-haps the most consequential chapter about the Messiah. This chapter describes the lengths to which the Messiah king goes to redeem mankind, and the nations, back to himself.

The context of the Isaiah 53 passage, begins with the last three verses of chapter 52:

> Behold, my servant shall act wisely;
> he shall be high and lifted up,
> and shall be exalted.
> As many were astonished at you—
> his appearance was so marred, beyond human semblance,
> and his form beyond that of the children of mankind—
> so shall he sprinkle many *nations*.
> Kings shall shut their mouths because of him,
> for that which has not been told them they see,
> and that which they have not heard they understand
> (Isaiah 52:13–16).

In this prophetic pericope, God's Messianic servant will be "high and lifted up and shall be exalted." God promised that his servant would be lifted up, a word derived from the Hebrew *nasa'*. This very word is used in Isaiah 2:2 as a description of the mountain of the Lord being lifted up as the nations flow to it. The exalted Messiah king, the ultimate suffering servant, would come to bring peace through his sacrificial death. Further, the nations of the world benefit from his selfless act.

The sprinkling of the nations (Hebrew, goyim) in Isaiah 52:15 is to be understood in context with Isaiah 53. Sprinkling

(Hebrew, nazah) is closely associated with the cleansing of sins in the Hebrew Scriptures (Exodus 24:8; Leviticus 3:6, Number 19:21, Ezekiel 36:25). A few observations are warranted. First, the suffering servant Messiah king would be offered up like a slaughtered lamb. Often the blood of the sacrificial lamb was sprinkled on the altar for sins to be atoned (Numbers 6:4; Leviticus 4:32; 2 Chronicles 29:20). Second, Jesus' slaughtered life served as an offering for guilt (Isaiah 53:10b). The offering referred to in this verse reminds us that his sprinkled blood would make the nations righteous. It is followed by what his sacrifice accomplished for "many" (which I believe is a reference to the nations). Isaiah 53:11 says, "Out of the anguish of his soul he shall see and be satisfied; by his knowledge shall the righteous one, my servant, make many to be accounted righteous, and he shall bear their iniquities." His imputed righteousness restores our standing before God.

The prophetic corpus of the Old Testament reveals God's desire to bring about the redemption of people from every tribe, tongue, and nation:

> Isaiah 25:6 – "On this mountain the LORD Almighty will prepare a feast of rich food for **all peoples**, a banquet of aged wine – the best of meats and the finest of wines."

> Isaiah 45:23 – "By myself I have sworn, my mouth has uttered in all integrity a word that will not be revoked: **Before me every knee will bow; by me every tongue will swear**."

> Isaiah 49:6 – "(The Lord) says: 'It is too small a thing for you to be my servant to restore the tribes of Jacob and bring back those of Israel I have kept. **I will also make you a light for the Gentiles, that you may bring my salvation to**

the ends of the earth.'"

Jeremiah 3:17 – "At that time they will call Jerusalem The Throne of the LORD, and **all nations will gather in Jerusalem to honor the name of the LORD. No longer will they follow the stubbornness of their evil hearts.**"

Daniel 7:14 – "He was given authority, glory and sovereign power; **all peoples, nations and men of every language worshipped him**. His dominion is an everlasting dominion that will not pass away, and his kingdom is one that will never be destroyed."

Zephaniah 2:11 – "The LORD will be awesome to them when he destroys all the gods of the land. **The nations on every shore will worship him, everyone in its own land.**"

Haggai 2:7 – "'**I will shake all nations, and the desired of all nations will come**, and I will fill this house with glory,' says the LORD Almighty."

Zechariah 9:10 – "I will take away the chariots from Ephraim and the war-horses from Jerusalem, and the battle bow will be broken. **He will proclaim peace to the nations**. His rule will extend from sea to sea and from the River to the ends of the earth."

Malachi 3:12 – "'**Then all the nations will call you blessed**, for yours will be a delightful land,' says the LORD Almighty."

Men and women from all earthly kingdoms, nations, peoples, and tribes will one day bow down to worship the Messiah King.

Daniel The Foreigner

Isaiah prophesied prior to God's people going into captivity. After his prophecies the people of Judah were captured and enslaved. The book of Daniel takes place during the time of captivity, the Babylonian exile. Daniel was a young man when he was exiled from Judah during the reign of Jehoiakim (Daniel 1:1). After the Babylonians conquered Judah, Daniel became a foreigner for the rest of his life. Further, Daniel lived in the most prosperous times of Babylon. He also lived beyond to the time when Babylon was overthrown by the Medo-Persian empire. But despite his captivity, Daniel the foreigner prospered. The book of Daniel demonstrates how God is completely in control over kings, empires, and kingdoms. Furthermore, it announces the coming of an everlasting kingdom that will have no end.

Daniel experienced the most common temptations of any young man when displaced to a foreign land. However, Daniel remained faithful to the Lord. The first part of the book, chapters one through six, among other things, contains the account of Daniel and three of his friends. These young men, who became foreigners in Babylon, are an example of spiritual steadfastness. They became examples of how God's people should live as foreigners, exiles, and strangers in a world that is not their own. Though they were surrounded by pagan culture their faith did not waver. One can be *in* the world, and not necessarily *of* the world. They took heed of to obey God. They took the words of the prophet Jeremiah seriously:

> Thus, says the Lord of hosts, the God of Israel, to all the exiles whom I have sent into exile from Jerusalem to Babylon: Build houses and live in them; plant gardens and eat their produce. Take wives and have sons and daughters; take wives for your sons, and give your daughters in marriage, that they may bear sons and daughters; multiply there, and do not decrease. *But seek the welfare of the city*

where I have sent you into exile, and pray to the Lord on its behalf, for in its welfare you will find your welfare (Jeremiah 29:4–7).

During the time in which the prophet Daniel lived, the majority of God's people were far from the Promised Land. For them, all hope was lost for Israel. Thankfully, God's plans do not fail, and neither do his promises. The hope of Israel turned to a Messianic king. He and his kingdom are announced in Daniel. He is the person about whom the prophets spoke, the one through whom God would establish his everlasting dominion.

Daniel prophesied about the Messiah in one of the most seminal Old Testament passages about God's kingdom:

I saw in the night visions, and behold, with the clouds of heaven, there came one like a son of man, and he came to the Ancient of Days and was presented before him. And to him was given dominion and glory and a kingdom, that all peoples, nations, and languages should serve him; his dominion is an everlasting dominion, which shall not pass away, and his kingdom one that shall not be destroyed (Daniel 7:13–14).

The words "son of man" became one of Jesus' favorite titles for himself in the New Testament. It appears 81 times throughout the four Gospels. It is this man, a Messianic kingly figure, that was going to come to rule over all earthly kingdoms. Even the Psalmist prophesied about his coming. In Psalm 2, the nations rage against him. He is described as king over Zion, God's holy mountain (Hebrew, *har*). Further, in Psalm 2 he is the Son to whom all kings and rulers are to submit to:

Now therefore, O kings, be wise; be warned, O rulers of the earth. Serve the Lord with fear and rejoice with trembling.

Kiss the Son, lest he be angry, and you perish in the way, for his wrath is quickly kindled. Blessed are all who take refuge in him (Psalm 2:10–12).

The son of man in the Old Testament is the Son of God. Daniel's description of the Messiah Jesus is astounding. He is given total dominion over all the earth. He is adorned with glory. And he is put in charge of a kingdom that yields power over all peoples, nations, and languages. His kingdom and rule are contrasted with Israel's and all other foreign nations. His kingdom is everlasting, and despite all best efforts, it shall never be destroyed! Furthermore, his kingdom will be shared with his saints or "holy ones" (Aramaic, *kaddish*, Daniel 7:22, 27).

Earlier in the book of Daniel, Nebuchadnezzar, the most powerful king of Babylon, attempted to subjugate the nations to himself. In Daniel chapter 3, he built himself a golden statue. He then commanded all peoples, nations, and languages to bow down to worship his self-image (Daniel 3:7). His intimidation attempt failed as Shadrach, Meshach, and Abednego refused to bow down before him, kindling his fury. However, his fury did not last long as God miraculously showed Nebuchadnezzar his power over the fiery furnace. God's deliverance led him to utter the following words:

> King Nebuchadnezzar to all peoples, nations, and languages, that dwell in all the earth: Peace be multiplied to you! It has seemed good to me to show the signs and wonders that the Most High God has done for me: How great are his signs, how mighty his wonders! His kingdom is an everlasting kingdom, and his dominion endures from generation to generation (Daniel 4:1–3).

Daniel the foreigner in his book sounded out a very clear message: God's kingdom shall be an everlasting kingdom, and all mankind shall serve and obey him! Those who submit to his rule will forever dwell him as heavenly citizens.

Ezra The Foreigner And Nehemiah The Foreigner

The people of God were living in Babylon during the writing of the book of Ezra. After the Babylonians were conquered by the Persians in 539 B.C., King Cyrus issued an edict allowing Jews to return to Jerusalem. Jewish foreigners who had been taken captive to Babylon were guaranteed freedom from exile. Ezra 1:11 records the return of Jewish exiles back to Judah through the leadership of Sheshbazzar who became the prince of Judah. The reason for the return? The rebuilding of the Jerusalem temple.

God chose Jerusalem as the place for his dwelling. The Old Testament constantly points to this location as the locus of worship for God's people. Cyrus recognized the importance of Jerusalem and purposed to rebuild God's temple in this location. Is it not fascinating? God used a foreigner as the main instrument to rebuild his temple.

The rebuilding of the temple was riddled with challenges. The remnants of Israel that returned to the land of Judah were challenged by the foreigners who had settled there during the exile period. When the Jews were ordered to return to Judah and build the temple they faced fierce foreign opposition. Ezra 4:4 records,

> Then the people of the land discouraged the people of Judah and made them afraid to build and bribed counselors against them to frustrate their purpose, all the days of

Cyrus king of Persia, even until the reign of Darius king of Persia (Ezra 4:4).

Despite the efforts of the foreign peoples who dwelt in the land of Judah, God's plan triumphed. And it is during this time that the prophets Haggai and Zechariah prophesied.

In Haggai, God lamented that his house was in ruins while his people dwelled in paneled houses (Haggai 1:2–4). God then used the prophet Haggai to speak words of encouragement to the faithful remnant who had returned to the land. Just like he told Joshua the foreigner to be strong and courageous after Moses' death, he told his people the Lord was with them and would be with them (Haggai 2:2-5; see also Zechariah 8:9-13).

God's redemptive purpose for the nations was continuing to advance. The nations would come to Jerusalem to worship him. His Messianic kingdom would be established as the nations would be stirred up, shaken (Hebrew, *ra`ash*), by the glory of God:

> For thus says the Lord of hosts: "Yet once more, in a little while, I will shake the heavens and the earth and the sea and the dry land. *And I will shake all nations*, so that *the treasures of all nations shall come in*, and I will fill this house with glory, says the Lord of hosts. The silver is mine, and the gold is mine, declares the Lord of hosts. The latter glory of this house shall be greater than the former, says the Lord of hosts. And in this place I will give peace, declares the Lord of hosts" (Haggai 2:6–9).

In addition to Haggai, the prophet Zechariah also announced the restoring Jerusalem, the holy dwelling of the Lord, the people of God, and his temple:

> Therefore, thus says the Lord, I have returned to Jerusalem

with mercy; my house shall be built in it, declares the Lord of hosts, and the measuring line shall be stretched out over Jerusalem. Cry out again, Thus says the Lord of hosts: "My cities shall again overflow with prosperity, and the *Lord will again comfort Zion and again choose Jerusalem*" (Zechariah 1:16–17).

Further, just as Haggai prophesied about the nations, so did Zechariah:

"Behold, I will *shake* my hand over them, and they shall become plunder for those who served them. Then you will know that the Lord of hosts has sent me. Sing and rejoice, O daughter of Zion, for behold, I come, and I will dwell in your midst, declares the Lord. And *many nations shall join themselves to the Lord in that day and shall be my people*. And I will dwell in your midst, and you shall know that the Lord of hosts has sent me to you. And the Lord will inherit Judah as his portion in the holy land and will again choose Jerusalem" (Zechariah 2:9–12).

The nations would be joined to God through the work of his servant, the Branch. The Branch is the Messianic king foretold by the other prophets. In Zechariah 3:8–10, the Lord prophesied to a lesser Joshua (son of Zerubbabel) about a greater Joshua (Jesus, the son of God) who would "remove the iniquity of this land in a single day." He would build the temple and rule on his throne as a peaceful ruler (Zechariah 6:12–13). This Messiah king would be greater than David and Solomon. He would be a perfect ruler whose kingdom would have no end, unlike his predecessors.

The everlasting dominion Daniel prophesied about would be fulfilled through him. Both Jews and Gentiles are partakers of the blessings of the Messiah king (Zechariah 8:20–23). He would come adorned as a righteous Savior king, riding on a donkey—

as Christ did in his triumphal entry into the city of Jerusalem, which is highlighted in all four Gospels (Matthew 21:1–11, Mark 11:1–11, Luke 19:28–44, and John 12:12–19) —bringing with him a message of peace to the nations:

> Rejoice greatly, O daughter of Zion! Shout aloud, O daughter of Jerusalem! Behold, your king is coming to you; righteous and having *salvation is he*, humble and mounted on a donkey, on a colt, the foal of a donkey. I will cut off the chariot from Ephraim and the war horse from Jerusalem; and the battle bow shall be cut off, and *he shall speak peace to the nations* his rule shall be from sea to sea, and from the River to the *ends of the earth* (Zechariah 9:9–10).

Zechariah announced the coming of one day when God would fully establish his everlasting rule. His message can be summarized in one verse, Zechariah 14:9, "And the Lord will be king over all the world. On that day the Lord will be one and his name one." Further, his redemptive work would begin in Jerusalem. Hence why the book of Ezra highlights the rebuilding of the temple after the Jewish exile. The former glory of Jerusalem began to be rebuilt. Enter, Nehemiah the foreigner.

Nehemiah was a Jewish foreigner who lived in the city of Susa under the rule of king Artaxerxes. Artaxerxes ruled over Babylon during the Second Temple period (the time when the second temple was rebuilt), and Nehemiah was his cupbearer. Nehemiah received word that Jerusalem was in ruins. The city had been desecrated and its walls were destroyed. After weeping, fasting and praying, God granted him an audience with the king who gave him permission to rebuild the city walls of Jerusalem.

Nehemiah faced foreign opposition the moment he

stepped foot in the land of Judah. Foreigners threatened him, "But when Sanballat the Horonite and Tobiah the Ammonite servant heard this, it displeased them greatly that someone had come to seek the welfare of the people of Israel" (Nehemiah 2:10). These two men and Geshem the Arab persecuted Nehemiah. They came to fight against the wall builders. However, they were not able to overcome (Nehemiah 4:7–9). Despite their opposition the construction of the city walls was not deterred. It was finished in merely fifty-two days (Nehemiah 6:15).

After the walls of Jerusalem and the temple were rebuilt, Ezra and Nehemiah led the Jewish foreign exiles into a season of revival. After the public reading of the Word, this revival led to repentance (Nehemiah 9:2). All revivals are accompanied by acts of repentance. Both the temple priesthood and the governance of Judah were restored back to the Jews, as God had promised though the prophet Jeremiah (Jeremiah 25:11).

A cleansing among God's people also occurred. Jewish foreign intermarriage was put to a stop. Intermarriage was forbidden because of idolatry, not on the basis of ethnicity. The Jewish people who lived in Judah had intermingled with foreigners. They married women from Ashdod, Ammon, and Moab. Nehemiah and Ezra both prohibited such acts from continuing in the land. Evoking king Solomon's mistake, they reminded the men of Judah of how the great king had been led astray by foreign women (Nehemiah 13:26–27). Ezra also led the marriage reformation. He opposed it because the men of Judah committed abominations against God through the influence of their foreign wives (Ezra 9:13).

Both the books of Ezra the foreigner and Nehemiah the foreigner end with the purging of foreign sin from the land of Judah. They led the charge for God's people to once again live like redeemed-foreigners. At the end of the book of Ezra, the priests repent and separate themselves from their foreign wives. Revival is fueled by both joyful and painful repentance. Nehemiah also prohibited trade on the Sabbath, which allowed foreigners to bring in food into Jerusalem on the most sacred day (Nehemiah 13:15–17). Nehemiah's task to cleanse the land from foreign evil was accomplished. He recounts,

> Thus, I cleansed them from everything foreign, and I established the duties of the priests and Levites, each in his work; and I provided for the wood offering at appointed times, and for the firstfruits. Remember me, O my God, for good (Nehemiah 13:30–31).

Esther The Foreigner

One final foreigner is worthy of mention. Hadassah, a Jewish foreign girl who lived during the days of Ezra and Nehemiah played an important role in the preservation of God's people during the exile. She is best known as Esther, her Persian-given name.

Esther belonged to the period after the Babylonian exile, when Persia had replaced Babylon as the ruling power. Her story, like Nehemiah's, takes place in the city of Susa, the Persian capital, during the reign of King Ahasuerus, better known by his Greek name, Xerxes I (486–464 B.C.). While some Jews had returned to the land of Judah, others like Esther and Mordecai (her uncle), were still in exile. The Jews were a minority group in Susa. As Ezra and Nehemiah encountered opposition from certain foreigners, so did Esther and Mordecai.

Haman, an Agagite foreigner, tried to annihilate the Jews.

He became known as the "enemy of the Jews" (Esther 3:10). The Agagites were foreigners who were descendants of the Amalekites. God told Saul to destroy all Amalekites, but he spared the life of Agag. Now, in the book of Esther, the Amalekites still posed a threat to the Jews. Interestingly enough, Mordecai, like king Saul, descended from Kish.

Haman served as a Satan-like figure within king Ahasuerus' court. He wanted to crush the seed of Abraham and destroy them. But his plans did not prevail. After Vashti, the foreign wife of Ahasuerus lost favor with the king, God used Esther to ensure his people did not perish. With the help of Mordecai, Esther's devout uncle, the Jews were able to survive and thrive in exile. Like Daniel and his friends, Esther and Mordecai sought the welfare of their city, as commanded in Jeremiah 29:4–7, and it was well with them.

The book of Esther demonstrates God's faithfulness to his people. It also shows us that God's plans will not fail despite any type of resistance. His salvific plans prevail. God's plan was to the Jew first. He preserved his people who were taken into foreign exile. He used people like Daniel, Ezra, Nehemiah, Esther, and others to ensure his plan succeeded. Why? Because salvation would come out of Judah. It would come from among the Jews.

The Jews, who were oppressed by foreigners, would become the conduit for the redemption of the nations, all foreigners. As Daniel and the prophets forecasted, God's redemptive plan is for both Jew and Gentile. His goal was, and still is, to bring all who will repent and believe in his name unto salvation. This truth is most profoundly evidenced in the New Testament, to which we now turn.

CHAPTER SIX

The Ultimate Foreigner

Arise, shine, for your light has come, and the glory of the Lord has risen upon you. For behold, darkness shall cover the earth, and thick darkness the peoples but the Lord will arise upon you, and his glory will be seen upon you. And nations shall come to your light, and kings to the brightness of your rising – Isaiah 60:1–3

Then he opened their minds to understand the Scriptures, and said to them, "Thus it is written, that the Christ should suffer and on the third day rise from the dead, and that repentance for the forgiveness of sins should be proclaimed in his name to all nations, beginning from Jerusalem – Luke 24:45–47

Guess what? Jesus died to save foreigners. I grew up in a Christian family. I learned about Jesus from an early age. My parents took us to church every week. Our worship services started at 7 PM and usually ended around 9. Most weeks, we left church around 10 PM. We were often the last people to leave church! I must admit I did not like that very much. However, I am thankful that my parents invested in our spiritual lives and pointed us to Christ.

Today I still remember many of the songs our Sunday

school teachers taught us. When I visit my home church in Brazil, my Sunday school teachers reminisce on the good old days they had teaching me, which was not an easy task! Let's just say I was not an exemplary child. Their dedication and passion for Christ was evident. They loved Christ and they loved me. For that I am truly grateful.

At church we were taught Old Testament history, the context of ancient biblical cultures, and the various stories of both the Old and New Testaments. Scripture was primary. But most importantly, we learned about Jesus Christ. We learned that Jesus died for us. However, it was not until later on that I understood the significance of Christ's earthly ministry. Jesus became an earthly foreigner so that we would no longer be foreigners to God! God's plan for redemption started in Genesis, and after the period between the Old and New Testaments the time for Jesus' arrival finally came.

The Intertestamental period (the time between the Old and New Testaments) lasted over four-hundred years. After the Jewish people resettled in the land of Israel, their struggles continued. Foreign nations continued to move around the region establishing their rule. As Daniel predicted, the Babylonians ruled for a while, then the Persians, the Greeks, and finally the Romans. Pompey of Rome conquered Israel around 63 BC, putting all of Judea under control of the Caesars. Herod, a foreign ruler, became king of Judea by the authority of the Roman emperor and senate. The Romans taxed and controlled the Jews. Roman, Greek, and Hebrew cultures were now mixed together in Judea.

During this time much of Jewish culture had changed. Most Jews became Hellenized. Most of them spoke Aramaic, Greek,

Hebrew, and some even spoke Latin. It is in this hodgepodge environment that Jesus entered human history. The promised "seed" arrived. The promised son of Man, the son of God, the Messiah king arrived on earthly territory as predicted by the prophets of old. 1 Peter 1:10–11 (NIV) says, "Concerning this salvation, the prophets, who spoke of the grace that was to come to you, searched intently and with the greatest care, trying to find out the time and circumstances to which the Spirit of Christ in them was pointing when he predicted the sufferings of the Messiah and the glories that would follow." Finally, the time of his arrival came.

Jesus The Foreigner

The Gospel of Matthew begins with a detailed genealogy of Jesus. Beginning with Abraham and then tracing Christ's family tree through king David, Matthew highlights Jesus' kingly roots. God had promised Abraham, "And I will make of you a great nation, and I will bless you and make your name great... and in you all the families of the earth shall be blessed" (Genesis. 12:2–3). Abraham's seed, or offspring, would be the conduit of Messianic promise fulfillment. Matthew intentionally began his gospel with a genealogy pointing to Abraham and David to show us the fulfillment of all Old Testament promises culminating in the person of Jesus.

Matthew begins with Abraham. Then he quickly moves to highlight the Davidic Covenant, which pinpointed the coming of the Messiah from one of the tribes of Israel––Abraham's son––the tribe of Judah. His rule and kingdom would be like no other. DeRouchie writes, "As the representative royal 'offspring' of

Abraham and David (Gen 22:17b–18; 2 Sam 7:12; Jer 33:26), the royal servant's faithful covenant obedience would secure new life for all who submit to his kingship (Isa 55:3–5), and these redeemed would then be counted 'his offspring' (53:10)—a children no longer desolate but now flourishing and expanded, having inherited the nations (54:1, 3; cf. Gen 28:14)."[31]

A closer reading of Matthew chapter one also shows the influence of foreigners like Tamar, Rahab, and Ruth in the lineage of Jesus. Beginning with Abraham who begat Isaac, all subsequent heads of family beget a new son (Matthew 1:2–15). In contrast, however, no human father begat Jesus, "Jacob [was] the father of Joseph the husband of Mary, of whom Jesus was born, who is called Christ (Matthew 1:16)."

The enigma is solved as Matthew immediately points out that Jesus was to be conceived of the Holy Spirit:

> Now the birth of Jesus Christ took place in this way. When his mother Mary had been betrothed to Joseph, before they came together *she was found to be with child from the Holy Spirit* (Matthew 1:18).

Matthew's genealogy highlights redemptive history from Abraham to the exile. Roy Ciampa writes,

> Matthew's opening genealogy (which structures the history of Israel around the key turning points of Abraham, David, the exile, and then the coming of Christ, so that the coming of Christ is to be understood as the key to the ultimate end of Israel's exile and the final restoration promised by the prophets, his quotation and interpretation of Isaiah 7:14 (and its evoking of the Immanuel theme of Isaiah), as well as the rest of the biblical interpretation that leads up to that verse.[32]

A miraculous birth indeed! The son of Man was conceived supernaturally. Fully God, fully human. He is both the Son of God and the Son of Man. The hypostatic union, fully God and fully human. He indeed came as a foreigner. Isaiah called him *Immanuel*, which means "God is with us." The unique son of God (John 3:16). God came to be with us:

> All this took place to fulfill what the Lord had said through the prophet: "The virgin will conceive and give birth to a son, and they will call him Immanuel" (which means "God with us") (Matthew 1:22–23).

Is there a more profound description of both Christ's otherness and his human similitude than *Immanuel*? God the Son came to dwell with men as a resident alien. He actually became one of us!! One like none other.

After his birth he was crowned king. However, instead of being crowned by his own people as king, foreign dignitaries came to crown him. Magi from the east arrived to greet him in Bethlehem of Judah. As John put it in his Gospel, "He came to his own and his own people did not receive him" (John 1:11). Jesus came not only to establish his kingdom over Israel, but all the nations of the earth.

At the end of the Gospel of Matthew Jesus commanded his disciples to make disciples of all nations (Matthew 28:18–20, the text famously known as the Great Commission). Their call was not just to proclaim the gospel among the Jewish people, but also among the Gentiles. In fact, Paul himself declared, "For I am not ashamed of the gospel of Jesus Christ for it is the power of God for salvation to everyone who believes, to the Jew first and also to the Greek" (Romans 1:16). The gospel is for all because God desires all to be saved. The gospel is for all foreigners, and invites all foreigners into redemption, making them into redeemed-foreigners. Matthew and the other disciples recognized this was their call. Alongside their witness, came a Gentile convert by the name of Luke.

Luke is responsible for writing one of the four Gospel accounts of the New Testament as well as the book of Acts. Luke's birth narrative demonstrates that he understood Christ's role. Jesus Christ was to come to fulfill the Davidic covenant. Christ came to usher his everlasting kingdom (Luke 1:29–33). The everlasting king, the royal Branch of David, the one who would carry government on his shoulders, the ruler of the everlasting monarchy prophesied by Daniel, arrived on earth in the form of a human baby:

> He will be great and will be called the Son of the Most High. And the Lord God will give to him the throne of his father David, and he will reign over the house of Jacob forever, and of his kingdom there will be no end (Luke 1:32–33).

The Prince of peace came to bring his "shalom" to Israel, and also to the whole earth. That's why the angels declared at his birth: "Glory to God in the highest heaven, and *on earth peace* to those on whom his favor rests" (Luke 2:14). Soon after his birth Jesus was taken to the temple. Another declaration highlights his impact upon the nations:

> [Simeon] took him up in his arms and blessed God and said, "Lord, now you are letting your servant depart in peace, according to your word; for my eyes have seen your salvation that you have prepared in the presence of all peoples a light for revelation to the Gentiles, and for glory to your

people Israel." (Luke 2:28–32).

Jesus encountered animosity from his own people, the Jews. After reading in the synagogue on a Sabbath day Jesus confronted those present. He made a point to highlight how Gentiles in the Old Testament had more faith in God than the devout Jews of his day (Luke 4:24–27).

Both the widow of Zarephath and Naaman the Syrian, foreign Gentiles, lived during a time of great apostasy in Israel. God's concern for the marginalized, especially foreign Gentiles, is a theme that runs through the Gospel of Luke. In fact, Luke is the only one who highlights Jesus' parable of the Good Samaritan.

In Luke 10:25–37, Jesus speaks to a lawyer about who should inherit eternal life. The conclusion is simple, those who love God will inherit eternal life. Jesus' message was simple: love God and love others. The man pressed Jesus further with the question, "Who is my neighbor"? The Pharisees preferred their own. They disdained the Gentile foreigners. Further, they disdained and despised the Samaritans. So, Jesus in clever fashion tells the man a parable.

The Samaritan foreigner of Jesus' parable was more righteous than a priest and a Levite. Such people were the most honored in Jewish society at that time. They were thought of as holy, pure, and righteous. Unlike other foreigners in Luke's Gospel (for example the widow of Zarephath and Naaman the Syrian in Luke 4:25–27 or the thankful Samaritan leper in Luke 17:12–19), the Good Samaritan is not the recipient of mercy, rather, like Jesus, he is one who shows mercy. Throughout Luke's Gospel Jesus shows compassion to the alienated—be they for-

eigners, prostitutes (Luke 7:36–50), beggars (16:19–31), desti-
tute widows (18:1–8), tax collectors (Luke 5:27–32; 18.9–14;
19:1–10), or alienated sons (15:11–32).

The theme around Christ the foreigner is found throughout Luke. A few observations are worth mentioning. First, at his
crucifixion a man named Simon the Cyrene helped him carry
the cross. Simon was a foreigner. Second, Jesus was crucified
as a foreigner. Hebrews 13:12 says, "So also Jesus suffered and
died outside the gate in order to sanctify the people his own
blood." He was crucified outside the city in a place called Gol-
gotha. Ironically, Pilate, a Roman foreigner, was responsible for
delivering Jesus to be crucified. Jesus' crucifixion taking place
outside of Jerusalem is reminiscent of an exiled king who did
not die in his proper place. His proper place was on the throne
of David within the city of Jerusalem. But instead, his kingship
was mocked.

Third, he was crucified by foreign Roman soldiers and the
inscription above his head contained the words "Jesus of Nazar-
eth, the King of the Jews" which were inscribed in three different languages––Aramaic, Latin, and Greek––(John 19:20). Jesus,
in other words, was crucified as a foreigner king. A king who
looked defeated, but who ultimately won through his resurrection. King Jesus is ultimately victorious. And there will be a
day when everyone on earth will bow down before his throne,
in heaven and on earth, and every tongue will confess Christ's
Lordship, to the glory of God the Father (Philippians 2:9–11).

Above all, it was Christ's death and resurrection that
marked the beginning of a new reality for those who believe. In
a sense, Hamilton writes, "The Gospels interpret the death and
resurrection of Jesus in these terms. It is as though his death is

the climactic moment of exile, the moment when the temple is destroyed (cf. John 2:19), and his resurrection begins the new exodus (cf. Luke 9:31)."[33] It is through Christ's work that non-redeemed foreigners turn into redeemed-foreigners who later become heavenly citizens.

One of the most common treatments foreigners experience is ostracism. Likewise, so did Jesus. Jesus came to his own, but his own did not receive him (John 1:11). He was persecuted by Herod (Matthew 2:16–18). He was rejected by his people in the synagogues (Luke 4:16–30). The second person of the God-head, the God of the universe, became an immigrant when he came to this world.

Furthermore, Jesus was not only an immigrant in coming to earth, but he was also an immigrant during his time on earth. As a child, Jesus and his family fled to Egypt. His family had to escape to a foreign country leaving behind their relatives, possessions, and culture. They had to communicate with other people using a different language. They ate different food and had to get used to different customs. His human dad, Joseph, had to leave his work as a carpenter and to find a job in a foreign land (Matthew 2:13–15,19–20).

The full restoration of peace between man and God is fulfilled in him. No longer strangers, those who believe in Christ by faith become citizens of his eternal kingdom. Hamilton expands, "Those who believe in Jesus have been saved through the salvation through judgment of the exile and restoration he accomplished in his death and resurrection, and we are now sojourning, passing through the wilderness on our way to the Promised Land, looking for that city with foundations, where the Lamb will be the lamp.[34]

The Message Of The Ultimate Foreigner

Jesus' message was clear. He came to announce the coming of the Kingdom of God. When dialoguing with Pilate, Jesus said, "My kingdom is not of this world. If my kingdom were of this world, my servants would have been fighting, that I might not be delivered over to the Jews. But my kingdom is not from the world" (John 18:36). The kingdom's arrival came in the form of the incarnate Son of God. The kingdom of God is the kingdom of Jesus Christ. He is its king. Even though his message was directed toward the Jews first, it also included the Gentiles. In fact, the arrival of the kingdom was prophesied by Isaiah who said,

> The people who walked in darkness
> have seen a great light;
> those who dwelt in a land of deep darkness,
> on them has light shone. (Isaiah 9:2).

He came as a light to the Jews and the Gentiles. Luke, alluding to Isaiah, also points out Jesus came as, "a light for revelation to the Gentiles, and for glory to your people Israel" (Luke 2:32).

Jesus came to show us the glory of God. He became like one of us. A sojourner who proclaimed the glories of the future kingdom. Robert Coleman writes, "This kingdom theme runs through Scripture. Of course, God is inherently King over all nations (2 Kings 19:15; Isaiah 6:5; Jeremiah 46:18), but in a special sense he was King of Israel (Exodus 15:17–18; Deuteronomy 33:5; Isaiah 43:15), working in their history to show his glory."[35] That is the reason why Christ went into the synagogues proclaimed he is the fulfillment of Messianic promises.

Though the kingdom arrived, it will only be fully established in a later time. Why? Because Christ is waiting for the right time when he will gather all his faithful ones from every corner of the planet. That is why our citizenship is not yet fully established. We will only enjoy its full benefits when in the presence of God in his eternal kingdom. Until then we are representatives of his kingdom on earth as redeemed-foreigners.

Christ said in Matthew 24:14, "And this gospel of the kingdom will be proclaimed throughout the whole world as a testimony to all nations, and then the end will come." In the same chapter Jesus also said a future time will come when all who believe in Christ will be gathered into his kingdom (more on this when we talk about the book of Revelation). How does one enter the kingdom? Not by good works and riches. We cannot purchase our entrance into the kingdom like we purchase something at a store. Rather, as Jesus said to the rich young ruler of Mark 10, kingdom acceptance hangs on the simple words, "follow me."

As it relates to the message of the kingdom, Christ's message concerning the kingdom is that the kingdom is open to both Jew and Gentile. In fact, there are two seminal texts that offer us great insight into his plan. First, there are the passages known as the Great Commission. While the Matthew passage is most often called the Great Commission, each Gospel and the Acts have a version of the commission of Jesus to go to the nations:

> And Jesus came and said to them, "All authority in heaven and on earth has been given to me. Go therefore and make disciples of all nations, baptizing them in the name of

the Father and of the Son and of the Holy Spirit, teaching them to observe all that I have commanded you. And behold, I am with you always, to the end of the age" – Matthew 28:18–20

And he said to them, "Go into all the world and proclaim the gospel to the whole creation. Whoever believes and is baptized will be saved, but whoever does not believe will be condemned" – Mark 16:15–16

And said to them, "Thus it is written, that the Christ should suffer and on the third day rise from the dead, and that repentance for the forgiveness of sins should be proclaimed in his name to all nations, beginning from Jerusalem. You are witnesses of these things" – Luke 24:46–48

These passages point to God's desire to gather people from all people groups around the world. The Greek phrase used for "all nations" in the Matthew passage is *panta ta ethne* in the original Greek text. This is an important expression; we are to go and make disciples "of all nations." *Ethne* is where we get the English word for "ethnicity." *Panta* means "all" or "every." Regarding this phrase John Piper writes,

We come back now to our earlier effort to understand what Jesus meant in Matthew 28:19 when he said, "Go and make disciples of *panta ta ethne*." This command has its corresponding promise of success in Matthew 24:14: "And this gospel of the kingdom will be proclaimed throughout the whole world as a testimony to all nations [*pasin tois ethnesin*], and then the end will come." The scope of the command and the scope of the promise hang on the meaning of *panta ta ethne*. My conclusion from what we have seen in this chapter is that one would have to go against the flow of the evidence to interpret the phrase *panta ta ethne* as "all Gentile individuals" (or "all countries"). Rather, the focus of the command is the discipling of all the people groups of the world.[36]

Second, before his ascension Jesus tells his disciples to focus on the task ahead. Their goal was not to know the time of his return. Rather, they were to become his witnesses and ambassadors, proclaiming the good news of salvation everywhere they went. Jesus told them,

> He said to them, "It is not for you to know times or seasons that the Father has fixed by his own authority. But you will receive power when the Holy Spirit has come upon you, and you will be my witnesses in Jerusalem and in all Judea and Samaria, and to the end of the earth" – Acts 1:7–8

Notice the following phrases: "make disciples of all nations," "Go into all the world and proclaim the gospel to the whole creation," "the forgiveness of sins should be proclaimed in his name to all nations," and "to the end of the earth." In the Gospel of John, Jesus uses the word "send" instead of "go." John's Gospel the commission is brief and to the point: "Peace be with you. As the Father has sent me, even so I am sending you" (John 20:21). As Jesus was sent, he now sends us. Where was Jesus sent? To all the world. To whom are we sent? To all the world. The implications are enormous. The gospel message is all-encompassing. It is to be proclaimed throughout the whole world to people groups from all nations. It is to be proclaimed to people, regardless of ethnicity, who were created in the image of God, for the glory of God.

All people are invited to be part of God's family, to worship him together as one, and to join him in the future as citizens of his heavenly kingdom. The church is not the kingdom, the church is not responsible for building the kingdom (God is), but rather its call is to bear witness to it.

Peter The Foreigner

The message of the kingdom of God was to be spread. And that is exactly what the disciples set out to do. Among them was a leader, Peter the foreigner. Peter was one of Jesus' most vocal disciples (i.e., Matthew 16:13–20). Upon Christ's ascension he became the leader among the 12 (Acts 1:15). On the Day of Pentecost, Peter lifted up his voice to preach the gospel. At the end of his life, he was sent to Rome where he was a foreigner.

At the gathering of the Jews in Jerusalem something extra-ordinary happened. Present in that place were Jews, devout men from "every nation under heaven" (*pantos ethnos,* Acts 2:5). At this special event, people began to speak in different tongues, and they understood each other! A miracle indeed (Acts 2:1–13). A miracle that marked the coming of the Holy Spirit upon God's people.

The Jewish exiles, foreigners, were gathered to celebrate the Feast of Weeks. At their gathering they experienced the power of God. Pentecost is the Greek name for the Hebrew Shavuot, which was the spring harvest festival of the Israelites. It was at Pentecost that the Holy Spirit came upon the early church believers. The Pentecost described in Acts 2 is a reversal of what happened at the tower of Babel. Medes, Persians, Mesopotamians, Romans, Arabs, were all present and everyone understood each other. The kingdoms Daniel prophesied about were all represented (cf. Daniel 2 and 7). Some of the people present were confused as to what was happening. But Peter stepped up to explain. Abraham's promise to be a blessing to all families was on full display.

Peter quoted the prophet Joel saying, "'And in the last days it shall be, God declares, that I will pour out my Spirit on all flesh" (Acts 2:17). He concludes his quotation of Joel by pointing out, "And it shall come to pass that EVERYONE who calls upon the name of the Lord shall be saved" (Acts 2:21). What an incredible message!!

Upon hearing Peter's words those present were astounded. Luke recounts, "Now when they heard this they were cut to the heart!" (Acts 2:37a). Peter then proceeded to tell them, "For the promise is for you and your children and for all who are far off, everyone whom the Lord our God calls to himself." In other words, all foreigners, all exiles, all who are far off are called unto repentance through Jesus Christ for the forgiveness of their sins. Peter and the disciples then baptized 3000 people that day, fulfilling their role as witnesses.

From that day onward, Peter became a staunch preacher to his foreign co-patriots. For instance, his first letter to the Christian believers begins with, "This letter is from Peter, an apostle of Jesus Christ. I am writing to God's chosen people who are *living as foreigners* in the provinces of Pontus, Galatia, Cappadocia, Asia, and Bithynia" (1 Peter 1:1, NLT). Nevertheless, Peter's witness was not limited to Jews. He boldly proclaimed the gospel in the temple at Jerusalem.

But one of his most significant tasks was yet to come. In Acts chapter 10, Peter is sent to a foreigner by the name of Cornelius. Cornelius is described as the Italian Cohort at Caesarea, "a devout man who feared God with all his household" (Acts 10:1–2). He was a Roman foreigner in Palestine. After receiving a vision from the Lord, Peter went to visit the man.

After meeting Cornelius, Peter understood the significance of what had just happened, though at first he did not. How could he have missed it? Did Jesus not tell him and the other disciples that they were to make disciples of all nations? Perhaps Peter thought Christ meant Jewish folks who lived in other nations, exiles, like the ones he had preached to in Acts 2. However, God's plans are bigger. After speaking with Cornelius Peter finally understood God's plan was not only for the Jews, but also for the Gentiles. He exclaimed,

> Truly I understand that God shows no partiality, *but in every nation [panti ethnos] anyone who fears him and does what is right is acceptable to him*. As for the word that he sent to Israel, preaching good news of peace through Jesus Christ —*He is Lord of all [panton kyrios]* (Acts 10:34–36).

The theme of the book of Acts is clear. Both Jews and Gentiles are called unto salvation. In fact, as Peter stated a few verses later that anyone and everyone who calls on the name of Jesus receives forgiveness (Acts 10:43). The Holy Spirit was poured out onto the Gentiles (Acts 10:45). Foreigners turned into redeemed-foreigners.

Furthermore, prior to the Gentile Pentecost with Cornelius in Acts 10, glimpses of salvation to the Gentiles began to appear. In Acts 8, the gospel was proclaimed in Samaria. Philip preached the word all over the region (Acts 8:4–5). He proclaimed the good news of the kingdom of God and the name of Jesus Christ. A foreign by the name of Simon is saved. And in the same chapter, Phillip proclaims the gospel to another foreigner, the Ethiopian Eunuch (Acts 8:27).

The Eunuch was reading a portion of the Isaiah scroll. He was confused. He needed someone to explain the meaning of the text to him. Phillip is sent by God to preach to him. After Phillip describes the text to the man he proclaimed his belief in Jesus Christ as the Son of God (Acts 8:3 7b). Perhaps, this man became the first gospel preacher to reach people in the country of Ethiopia.

Peter's call to repentance was also a call to holiness. He too understood we are all foreigners. And as redeemed-foreigners, our conduct must reflect our kingdom identity. That is why he wrote,

> *But you are a chosen race, a royal priesthood, a holy nation, a people for his own possession,* that you may proclaim the excellencies of him who called you out of darkness into his marvelous light. Once you were not a people, but now you are God's people; once you had not received mercy, but now you have received mercy. Beloved, I urge you as sojourners [foreigners – Greek *paroikos*] and exiles to abstain from the passions of the flesh, which wage war against your soul. Keep your conduct among the Gentiles honorable, so that when they speak against you as evildoers, they may see your good deeds and glorify God on the day of visitation (1 Peter 2:9–12).

As Peter and the other disciples preached and all the believers witnessed (see Acts 4:29–31; 8:1–4), the gospel continued to spread. Acts chapters 8 to 11 show how the gospel spread beyond Jerusalem to Judaea, Samaria, and Antioch in Syria, which at that time was the third most important city in the Roman Empire. The disciples were faithful in their gospel proclamation. However, it was Paul, a Jewish/Greek foreigner who witnessed the good news among the Gentile foreigners more significantly.

Paul The Foreigner

Paul was a devout Jew from Tarsus in Cilicia. In the first century, the city of Tarsus belonged to the Romans (Acts 21:39; 22:25). This means that Paul was both a Jew and a Roman. I can somewhat relate to this because I am both a Brazilian and an American. He was a foreigner everywhere he went. His devotion led him to persecute the Christians. However, God changed his life's trajectory in dramatic fashion. He too became a Christian.

In Acts 9, Jesus appeared to Paul. This appearance, called a theophany, left him perplexed (Acts 9:1–9). Jesus then appeared in a vision to Ananias. In this vision Jesus commands him, "But the Lord said to him, "Go, for he is a chosen instrument of mine *to carry my name before the Gentiles* and kings and the children of Israel" (Acts 9:15). And indeed, Paul shared the good news of Jesus throughout the region to both Jews and Gentiles. He was bold. He suffered a great deal, but he proclaimed the gospel with fervor. Why? Because he was not ashamed of the gospel, which is the power of God unto salvation to both Jew and Gentile (Romans 1:16–17).

Paul shared the gospel in the synagogues. In his first missionary journey he shared the gospel in the Jewish Synagogues of Cyprus (Acts 13). In his second missionary journey he preached in the region of Galatia. He also preached in Ephesus where Lydia, a Greek foreigner described as a "worshipper of God" (Acts 16:14) became a Christ follower. Paul's work among foreigners was extensive. Many of the people mentioned in his close circle were foreigners from diverse places like Thessalonica, Derbe, and Asia (Acts 20:3).

Paul was relentless in his gospel witness. He preached the gospel to the Gentiles (Romans 15:18–21). He preached before kings (Acts 26). He also preached among the Jewish people. As a matter of fact, at the very end of the book of Acts he told his Jewish brethren, "Therefore let it be known to you that this salvation of God has been sent to the Gentiles; they will also listen" (Acts 28:28). He knew his calling and testified to it,

> Paul, a servant of Christ Jesus, called to be an apostle, set apart for the gospel of God, which he promised beforehand through his prophets in the holy Scriptures, concerning his Son, who was descended from David according to the flesh and was declared to be the Son of God in power according to the Spirit of holiness by his resurrection from the dead, Jesus Christ our Lord, through whom we have received grace and apostleship to bring about the obedience of faith for the sake of his name among all the nations [*pasin tois ethnesin*] (Romans 1:1–5).

Beyond Paul's ministry to foreigners, he also understood he was a foreigner. He understood that as a redeemed-foreigner, his citizenship is in heaven. He wrote, "But our citizenship is in heaven, and from it we await a Savior, the Lord Jesus Christ" (Philippians 3:20). This world is simply the beginning. Eternity awaits us. The person who was previously alienated from God, a stranger, becomes a citizen of the kingdom of God.

In the book of Ephesians, Paul points out that Gentile believers, prior to Christ, had no hope in partaking of the blessings of God. But their reality changed through the blood of Christ. He writes,

> Therefore, remember that at one time you Gentiles in the

flesh, called "the uncircumcision" by what is called the circumcision, which is made in the flesh by hands—remember that you were at that time separated from Christ, *alienated* from the commonwealth of Israel and *strangers* to the covenants of promise, having no hope and without God in the world. But now in Christ Jesus you who once were far off have been brought near by the blood of Christ (Ephesians 2:11–13).

In addition to "alienated" Paul uses the word "stranger" to describe Gentile believers. This is the Greek word *xenos*. This is where we get the English term "xenophobia," a term associated with disdain or fear of foreigners. It is here that the preposition "but" becomes so important. "But now in Christ Jesus," says Paul. We are brought near by the blood of Christ. In other words, we are no longer estranged from God. Paul concludes a few verses later stating, "For through him we both have access in one Spirit to the Father. *So, then you are no longer strangers and aliens*, but you are fellow citizens with the saints and members of the household of God" (Ephesians 2:18–19).

Regardless of whether or not some refuse to worship Jesus, one day all will inevitably bow down before him. He will bring all under submission, whether they have been redeemed or not (Philippians 2:9–11). Redeemed-foreigners will enjoy the benefits of heavenly citizenship, while non-redeemed foreigners will inherit hell for eternity.

Another passage that shows Paul's commitment to other-worldly living is found in Colossians chapter 3. He wrote, "If then you have been raised with Christ, seek the things that are above, where Christ is, seated at the right hand of God. Set your minds on things that are above, not on things that are on earth" (Colossians 3:1–2). Note the focus on the person of Christ. Paul knew that the things of this world would take our minds away from heavenly things. That is why he encouraged the saints at Colossae to keep seeking and keep their minds on things above. As C. S. Lewis put it in his *Weight of Glory*, "Like an ignorant child who wants to go on making mud pies in a slum because he cannot imagine what is meant by the offer of a holiday at the sea. We are far too easily pleased."[37]

Paul also clung to a future hope in his sufferings. He focused on the prize he would one day receive from Christ. Using a metaphor, Paul describes how runners and boxers compete to win a prize. He correlates the idea of competing to win to help encourage Christ followers. However, he understood the prize that awaits Christ followers is much better. These athletes competed to win a crown, much like athletes today compete to win a trophy or a medal. But the difference is that the believer's crown is eternal. He points out, "They do it to get a crown that will not last, but we do it to get a crown that will last forever" (1 Corinthians 9:24–27). Charles Spurgeon once said, "There are no crown-wearers in heaven who were not cross-bearers here below."[38] Paul exemplifies this resolve.

He knew God had rescued him from the domain of darkness and brought him into the kingdom of the Son whom he loves (Colossians 1:13–14). That is why he remained steadfast amid his earthly trials.

As aliens on earth, we are called to set an example of what it means to live as if we do not belong to this world, but to God. We are called to represent Christ as his ambassadors. Paul knew we are all "ambassadors for Christ" (2 Corinthians 5:20). Until the day comes when we are in the presence of God, we are called to represent him, walk in his ways while on earth, and invite others to join our journey to the ultimate destination. And that is the topic of our next chapter.

CHAPTER SEVEN

The Ultimate Destination

Christ followers are redeemed-foreigners
on a pilgrimage to heaven

*There is a city built on high, From earthly sorrows free,
Bought by a Savior's precious blood, A home for you and
me. Its gates are pearl, its streets are gold, Its walls are
jewels rare. No need of sun or moon to shine, For God is
brightness there – The Celestial City, by Grace Watkins*

Guess what? "If you don't know where you are going,
you will end up someplace else," Yogi Berra once
noted. I remember when I first arrived in America for
the first time as a tourist. I barely spoke any English. I arrived
in America in December, shortly after the terrorist attack on
09/11/2001. The experience was overwhelming.

First, I had no clue where I was supposed to go upon arrival. I kept following the arrows on signs. Second, there was
no one who spoke Portuguese around me. It was like entering a
new dimension altogether. Third, the Dallas-Fort Worth airport
was filled with military personnel walking around with Ak-47s
wrapped around their bodies looking at everyone with suspicion. Finally, going through customs was also extremely taxing.

Let's just say many of the border patrol immigration officers look very intimidating, to put it mildly!

After customs I was supposed to go to baggage claim. But soon I realized I was lost inside the DFW airport. I did not know where I was supposed to go. After a little while, I heard a lady speaking in Spanish; I communicated with her to figure out which direction I should head. I arrived at my final destination and at last all was well.

Most people wander through life not knowing what their final destination is. Our final destination is not earth, at least not this earth as it is currently. And for that I am thankful. God, in his great mercy, has prepared a place called heaven for us to dwell with him for eternity. He has provided the map to our destination (the Bible), given us permission to arrive safely there (by faith), and procured our way in (Jesus).

Have you followed the progression thus far? We are all destined to arrive somewhere. The question we need to ask ourselves is, What will my final destination be?

God created us to live in perfect fellowship with him. He placed mankind in the Garden of Eden where he walked with them. After the Fall, things spiraled out of control. Evil entered his perfect creation and shattered all hope for peace. But God's compassion never ceases. He chose for himself a people from whom his redemption would be accomplished. He established his place of worship on a mountain in the city of Jerusalem.

The Israelites built the temple on earthly Mount Zion. This location became the place where his holy presence dwelt for a long time, and it is there all peoples are called to worship the triune God. It is the ultimate destination. But in its earthly state, Mount Zion, is imperfect. In fact, Jerusalem, where Mount

Zion is located has been conquered, battered, and destroyed over and over again. But there is a reality beyond this world: a new Jerusalem. An eternal destination reserved for those whose hope is in the Son of God, Jesus Christ.

The heavenly Mount Zion is the place where all the nations of the earth will gather to worship the Lord. Hebrews 12:22 says, "But you have come to Mount Zion and to the city of the living God, the heavenly Jerusalem, and to innumerable angels in festal gathering." God's final plan includes the glorification of himself through the worship of all peoples. Our worship now is merely a precursor for our future heavenly reality. Justo González calls it a rehearsal. He writes,

> Worship is also an act of rehearsal. It is an anticipation of things to come. It is the moment at which we are reminded that our lives and our world have a goal, and that this goal is that day when every nation and tribe and people and language will worship God and the Lamb. It must be a foretaste, within our small community of worship of that great city, the New Jerusalem, which John saw coming from heaven, from God. It is practice for the Kingdom. It is a foretaste of the reign of God.[39]

The new Jerusalem, the holy city, is the place all saints yearn for, no matter where they are from or when in history they lived. The church made up of redeemed-foreigners waits with great expectation for the day they will be able to enjoy being in the very presence of God as heavenly citizens. No longer strangers, we will be at home. The apostle Peter writes, "But according to his promise we are waiting for new heavens and a new earth in which righteousness dwells" (2 Peter 3:13). The author of Hebrews also exclaimed, "For here we have no lasting city, but we seek the city that is to come" (Hebrews 13:14).

In the New Testament, the book of Hebrews often points to this future place. In Hebrews 11, the saints of old are depicted as strangers and foreigners who longed for the heavenly city. Their eternal perspective is astounding. Even before the prophets spoke of the place, they knew about it! They longed for it,

> These all died in faith, not having received the things promised, but having seen them and greeted them from afar, and having acknowledged that they were strangers and exiles on the earth. For people who speak thus make it clear that they are seeking a homeland. If they had been thinking of that land from which they had gone out, they would have had the opportunity to return. But as it is, they desire a better country, that is, a heavenly one. Therefore, God is not ashamed to be called their God, for he has prepared for them a city (Hebrews 11:13–16).

In a sense, the Bible communicates to us that the best is indeed yet to come. That is why we should not be enamored with the things of this world. Akin writes, "God does not promise Christians their best life now; he promises our best life later...The Bible is clear that godliness is no guarantee that things will go well for us in this life. The Bible is equally clear that for those who follow Christ, things will go well ultimately for you in the next life."[40] Our expectation for this heavenly place must never wane!

No Longer Strangers – "I Will Be Their God And They Shall Be My People"

Both the Old and New Testaments point to a future reality. God desired to have a people for himself. There will come a future time when God will finally rule over his people. In the Torah, we see the echoes of God's intentions in Genesis and Exodus. When speaking to Abraham God declared that the covenant he established with him and his offspring would be an everlasting covenant (Genesis 17:7).

Note that God's intention was to establish an "everlasting covenant." His covenant was to continue to all eternity, not just temporarily on earth through Abraham's seed until he became a great nation. After Abraham's offspring multiplies, the Lord delivered them from slavery through Moses. Over one thousand years later, God speaks through the prophets Jeremiah and Ezekiel. Once again declares his desire for his people, pointing to the Messianic covenant,

> For this is the covenant that I will make with the house of Israel after those days, declares the Lord: I will put my law within them, and I will write it on their hearts. And I will be their God, and they shall be my people (Jeremiah 31:33).

Perhaps the best summary of God's desire to establish a group of redeemed-foreigners to worship him forevermore in the prophets is found in Ezekiel 37:22–28, It concludes with this promise:

> *My dwelling place shall be with them, and I will be their God, and they shall be my people.* Then the nations will know

that I am the Lord who sanctifies Israel, when my sanctuary is in their midst forevermore (Ezekiel 37:27–28).

These passages point to a future time where the kingdom of God will be fully established through the rule of his Messiah king. Furthermore, that is exactly what the author of the book of Hebrews points to in Hebrews 8:8–12. The words "I will be their God and they shall be my people" appear in verse 10, echoing the prophets. In the Old Testament, redemptive history focuses on Israel's responsibility to glorify God and bless the nations, while in the New Testament, redemptive history centers on the church's responsibility to proclaim God's glory to the nations.[41]

Fast forward to the book of Revelation. Revelation 21:3 declares that God will dwell with humanity. The final chapter in history concludes God's plan to restore fellowship with mankind. Bruce Ashford points out that it is here that God's plan for creation comes full circle. He writes, "The God who gave us the good creation recorded in Genesis narrative is the God who will give us a new heavens and a new earth."[42] Old Eden is restored into a new Eden. Hamilton puts it this way, "This new heaven and earth is a new and better Eden. The return from the exile from Eden has finally been fulfilled."[43]

Is it not interesting that the last book of the Bible is written by yet another foreigner? The Apostle John was exiled to the Island of Patmos during the rule of Emperor Domitian. John had walked, talked, and dined with Jesus. But his most profound encounter with Christ happened on the Greek island of Patmos. In his visions he was given a glimpse of what is to come. It is in the final pages of Scripture that John the foreigner reiterates

God's plan to bring all nations to this ultimate destination. The place? The holy city, the new Jerusalem (Revelation 21:1). The purpose? God's dwelling place is now among his people (Revelation 21:3). The result? No more suffering, no more pain (Revelation 21:4).

From Foreigners To Citizens

In Christ, those who were once enemies (Ephesians 2:1–5) are now children and co-heirs of God's promises (Colossians 3:21–22), including heaven. All who are redeemed by him are partakers of heavenly blessings. We move from being foreigners to God to becoming foreigners to the world system. Moreover, those who are Christ's are seated above in heavenly places (Ephesians1:3; 2:6). He turned those who come to him by faith from foreigners to redeemed-foreigners, and ultimately to heavenly citizens. Paul points out that Christ has reconciled believers though his body of flesh by his death, so that we would be presented before the Father holy and blameless and above reproach. Why? because we were alienated from God and hostile in mind toward God. But our evil deeds were ratified by his selfless sacrifice on the cross, which purchased our redemption (Colossians 1:21–22).

On the flip side, the reality of those who stand against God is stark. Those who do not repent and submit to his Lordship will be exiled for eternity. Jesus himself said, "Whoever believes in the Son has eternal life, but whoever rejects the Son will not see life, for God's wrath remains on them" (John 3:36). Hell is a terrible place of exile. Non-redeemed foreigners will spend eternity in exile.

Most people think this world will last forever. But it will not. One day the new heavens and the new earth will be established. And we have to make a choice. Will we choose to dwell with God in his everlasting heavenly kingdom or in hell away from his presence? Do not be mistaken, hell is permanent exile from God's loving presence. According to Scripture hell will be a place of torment, gnashing of teeth, and suffering (Daniel 12:2,3; Matthew 13:50; 25:46; John 5:28; Revelation 14:11; 20:14,15).

Now, before you think that God is unjust for condemning people to hell, remember that he provided a way out of it! In fact, he is preparing a heavenly dwelling of eternal bliss for those who believe in Jesus (John 3:16,17; 2 Corinthians 5:14,15; 1 Timothy 2:6; 4:10; Titus 2:11; 2 Peter 3:9). He wishes for all to come to repentance. And such salvation is for all people. How can we know? Well, the book of Revelation confirms it.

In Revelation we are given a snapshot of a future day when people from every tribe, language, people, and nation will gather around his throne to worship him in the new city Jerusalem (Revelation 5:9–10; Revelation 7:9–12). Philip O. Hopkins is correct to point out, "God's assurance that he will save people from all tribes, tongues, peoples, and nations is (or ought to be) near and dear to every Christian's heart."[44] John the foreigner testifies,

> After this I looked, and behold, a great multitude that no one could number, from every nation, from all tribes and peoples and languages, standing before the throne and before the Lamb, clothed in white robes, with palm branches in their hands, and crying out with a loud voice, "Salva-

tion belongs to our God who sits on the throne, and to the Lamb!" (Revelation 7:9–10).

There will be a future gathering of foreigners. Some will be gathered unto eternal life and some to eternal separation from God. Foreigners are invited to become citizens of heaven. But the gathering of heavenly citizens is reserved only for those whose citizenship has been granted by faith in the Lamb, Jesus Christ.

Remember the progression?

The new Jerusalem will be the place where the saints will live in eternal ecstasy. God will radiate his glory in such a way that he himself will be its light. There will be no more darkness, no more pain, no mourning, no suffering, no sin. Hamilton summarizes,

> At long last, the king [will come] with healing in his hands, succeeding where Adam and Israel failed, dying on behalf of his people, rising from the dead in triumph, and building a new temple—not a building but a body of believers (e.g., Eph. 2:19–22; 1 Pet. 2:4–5). This new temple is to be built from people of all nations, but the building of this temple is not the consummation of God's purposes. God's purposes will be realized when all see Jesus coming with the clouds, even those who pierced him, and they will mourn for him as one mourns for an only son, while the redeemed rejoice (Rev. 1:7; Zech. 12:10). He will then ascend the throne and judge the living and the dead (Revelation 19–20), and the dwelling of God will be with men in the new and better Eden, the new creation (Revelation 21–

22). God and the Lamb will be the temple (21:22). There will be no need for sun or moon, for the Lamb will be the lamp of God's glory, radiating light aplenty, the center-piece of praise (21:23–24).[45]

Jesus said he would draw all people to himself (John 12:32). But it does not mean that all people will dwell with him for-ever. The wicked will be judged. Those not covered by his blood will suffer eternally damning consequences (John 3:18). There will be a future day of reckoning. No one knows its exact arrival (Matthew 24:36). But it will certainly come. I'm reminded of the famous hymn written by James M. Black titled "When the Roll is Called Up Yonder,"

> When the trumpet of the Lord shall sound,
> and time shall be no more,
> And the morning breaks, eternal, bright and fair
> When the saved of earth shall gather over on the other shore,
> And the roll is called up yonder, I'll be there
> When the roll, is called up yonder,
> When the roll, is called up yonder,
> When the roll, is called up yonder,
> When the roll is called up yonder I'll be there

The question we all need to individually answer is, will I be there? I plan on it, and I hope you do as well! Foreigners no more!

Illustration by Sarah Lynn Miller
Revelation 21:2 and Revelation 22:1-2 – "The Heavenly City of Jerusalem"

People from every tribe, tongue, nations, and people headed to the heavenly city. Followers of Christ approaching the New City, and the overflowing tree of life with rivers of living water flowing over the Lamb of God's crown of thorns. In the beginning, the tree of life was mentioned and now, in the roots, the tree of life reflects its maturity, growth and strength. Eden is restored and redeemed-foreigners are fully instated as heavenly-citizens. The living waters flow as the waterfall from the garden now thru the tree of life, the fruits and the leaves are for the healing of all nations. He is the Alpha and Omega.

PART TWO

How Then Shall We Live?

These concluding three chapters hope to give you some practical insight on living as a redeemed-foreigner in this life.. Christians are called to live as ambassadors for Jesus on earth. How we understand our relationship with God and this world is vital; however, our conduct matters as well. Peter said our conduct needs to be "holy" and "godly" (2 Peter 3:11–12). Both these words refer to a different way of living than the world's. Since we have been set apart for God (chosen as citizens of his kingdom), we are to live in such a way that the world thinks we are foreigners. But not just foreigners, redeemed-foreigners. Since we have been redeemed by him, we should live in a way that is God-like, so that others observe our actions and give glory to him (Matthew 5:16).

    Peter also told us that since we are foreigners, we should resist the desires of the flesh (1 Peter 2:11). Paul phrases the concept differently in Ephesians 2:19, where he says we are no longer aliens. Is there a contradiction with Peter? There is not. Though they stand in contrast, they are not in opposition: we are both citizens of heaven (Paul's point) while at the same time we are foreigners wandering on earth (Peter's point) until Christ returns.

If we are not from this world, how then shall we live?

The next three chapters will focus on the family, society, and church.

CHAPTER EIGHT

Family

*But you are a chosen race, a royal priesthood, a holy
nation, a people for his own possession, that you may proclaim the excellencies of him who called you out of darkness into his marvelous light. Once you were not a people,
but now you are God's people; once you had not received
mercy, but now you have received mercy – 1 Peter 2:9–10*

G uess What? All redeemed-foreigners will one day be
part of God's heavenly family, dwelling in his presence
forever as heavenly citizens. One of the biggest challenges most foreigners face is being away from family. As of
now, I have spent half of my lifespan in Brazil, and the other half
in America. Before marriage, and to some extent until present,
I longed to be with my family. I longed to be home.

Holidays were particularly difficult. I had to spend many
holidays away from my loved ones. This created an emotional
void. I was fortunate enough to grow up in a loving family. My
home was always a place of refuge. We welcomed friends and
relatives almost every day of the week at our house. My parents
generously shared their possessions with others. My father and
my mother modeled godliness in their relationship with each
other and with God. In a sense, I grew up in a "normal" family

household. By normal I mean, the way God intended the family to be.

God instituted the family. The family was God's creation. In the beginning, after creating man and woman in his image, God told them to go forth and multiply (Genesis 1:28). The intent was to fill the earth with divine image bearers who worship their creator. God created the family to be a reflection of himself. As God the Father, Son, and Holy Spirit experience sweet fellowship, he designed us for fellowship.

After the Fall, the family nucleus was broken. Since then, sin has wreaked havoc within families everywhere. The result? Disobedience to parents, divorce, adultery, polygamy, dysfunctional relationships between relatives, and much more. Perhaps you grew up in a dysfunctional family. What are you to do?

The ultimate foreigner had an earthly family. Jesus who was born of Mary was also raised by her husband Joseph. He was submissive to them. As he submitted to them he increased in wisdom and stature, and in favor with God and men (Luke 2:51). As God, Jesus did not have to submit to the parents he actually created, but as man he chose to humble himself and obey them.

As God intended it, the nucleus of the family includes the relationship of husband to wife, and parents to child/children. It also relates to our extended families, as when Paul told Timothy (1 Timothy 5:4). Again, the percentage of broken families is extremely high in all societies. It is a result of the Fall. It is the reality of foreigners who live in a broken world. Sin distorted God's intended plan. Nevertheless, we are all called to submit to authority, both human and divine.

Husbands And Wives

I met my wife in college. I was immediately interested in her. However, to my shame I was already enamored with another girl. I think most folks who desire to be married one day struggle to find the best suitable companion. I wondered most of my life about whom I would marry. I never knew she would be so close to me while I had my arms around another girl! But thank God for his grace and mercy. Though I did not know Ashli would eventually become my wife when we first met, God's plans superseded my expectations beyond imagination. We have been married for almost 15 years and have three beautiful boys.

I have officiated a couple of dozen weddings in the past 15 years of ministry. It is one of my favorite things to do. Ashli accompanied me to almost every wedding I have officiated. I enjoy it, partly, because she looks beautiful every time we participate in these celebrations. Never mind the fact that at times we get to dance during wedding receptions, one of her favorite things to do. I enjoy dancing, but not as much as she does! Further, I get the opportunity to bless couples, but in turn I am blessed in return. I am deeply thankful for my marriage and wife, and the privilege to share life, laughter, tears, goals, struggles, and much more. But the most significant impact on my life and marriage comes from reflecting on what Scripture says about marriage.

In the beginning God created man and woman, male and female. When a marriage occurs, the two become one (Genesis

1:27; 2:23–24). Married couples were to become a reflection of God as they went forth and multiplied, increasing God's image in the world even more. David Jones writes, "As marriage partners experience their own one flesh existence, then, and as they meditate upon the reality of such, the composite unity of the Godhead should become less obscure. Indeed, the institution of marriage is likely the most practical and effective teaching aid in Scripture that assists mankind in understanding the truth that God is triune in essence."[46] Husband and wife were to be witnesses of God's own triune fellowship. But sin, like a terrible cancer, destroyed the beauty of perfect human fellowship.

In Genesis 3, God told Eve her rebellion would lead to labor pains and increase her desire to rule over her husband. In other words, women struggle submitting to their husbands for they are naturally inclined to rule over them, according to the curse pronounced in Genesis 3:16. John Macarthur points out, "Sin has turned the harmonious system of God-ordained roles into distasteful struggles of self-will. Lifelong companions, husband and wives, will need God's help in getting along as a result."[47]

Men were given the "curse of the ground." What does it mean? God intended for work to be pleasing, fulfilling, and good for men. They were working before the Fall! But because of his rebellion, now they would be burdened by the very thing that was supposed to bring them some significance.

In Ephesians 5, the apostle Paul reminds husbands and wives that their relationship is to be a reflection of Christ's own sacrificial love. Husbands are to love, to lead, and to protect their wives, and wives are to respect and to submit to their husbands (Ephesians 5:22–33). Love and respect are to be the fuel that fires up the engines of marriages.

Peter also understood husbands and wives were to live in such a manner. However, Peter frames his advice to husbands and wives in light of their standing as foreigners. In 1 Peter 2:11–12, the apostle urges believers to "abstain from the passions of the flesh." Their conduct was to be honorable, their deeds good, so that God would be glorified.

He encouraged believing wives to be respectful and pure in conduct. Likewise, he told husbands to be understanding, showing them honor because they too are kingdom citizens. The goal? Peter tells us, "Finally, all of you, have unity of mind, sympathy, brotherly love, a tender heart, and a humble mind. Do not repay evil for evil or reviling for reviling, but on the contrary, bless, for to this you were called, that you may obtain a blessing" (1 Peter 3:8–9).

How can husbands and wives love and respect each other? Rachel Pace, a blog writer offers some helpful advice for both husbands and wives:[48]

Husbands

1. *Show affection* - She needs hugs, kisses, cuddles, and loving touches. She needs to know that you love her in this way without it having to lead to intimacy every time.

2. *Give her lots of attention* - Women want a lot of attention. This can be shown in many ways, and it's essential to pay attention to what your wife truly needs. So, ask how her day went, show an interest in what she did that day, ask questions about what she thinks about particular issues to express your respect and love in marriage.

3. *Listen without giving advice* - Women need your listening ear. Women are smart, capable people. They can figure out their problems pretty well. But they need your encouragement to do so. If you have been wondering how to show love and respect in marriage, listen, instead of trying to solve their problems.

4. *Plan alone time, just the two of you* - Husbands, your wives crave time with only the two of you together. So, remember that couples time is synonymous with love and respect in marriage for a woman. Schedule date nights and at times do some impromptu hang out times together.

5. *Help her with the daily chores* - Nothing is more potent in showing love than helping your lady love with her daily tasks.

Wives

1. *Ask his opinion* - A man feels valued and respected when his thoughts are valuable to you. Wives don't make all the decisions with kids and the house on your own. Ask his opinion.

2. *Tell him what you appreciate about him* - He goes to work every day and deals with long hours and a lot of issues. He is good at helping things run smoothly there. At home, he helps the kids get to bed, and then he takes care of maintaining the lawn. One thing that shows a man you respect him is to tell him all of these things that you appreciate about him. Tell him you understand how hard he works.

3. *Use a loving tone* - When you are thinking about how to build respect in a marriage, a big part of respect to a man isn't just the content of the words, but how they are said. A man can spot insincerity or an unloving tone from a mile

away.

4. *Tell others about him* - What you say about your husband to others has a way of getting back to him. If it's good, he'll feel respected by you. Because when he's not near, and you are speaking well of him to others, he feels safe and good that you went to that effort.

5. *Believe in him* - Your husband needs your encouragement. Sometimes he feels vulnerable or unsure; if his wife is right there and believes he can do it, then that's all he needs. He will feel respected and will have the courage he needs to forge ahead.

Parents And Children

We all have something in common: we were born of our human mothers. Today, technology allows for surrogate mothers to couples who cannot bear children, and it also allows for lesbian or gay male couples to "have children." The various manifestations of parenting in our world are beyond the scope of this book. However, one thing is for sure, from a biblical standpoint God designed parenting to be the loving relationship of a father and mother to their biological children. To many who have not had the privilege of being raised by their biological parents, God gave the blessing of adoption. Our world is broken, but God's grace often shines through the love of adopted parents to their children.

Note that I qualified relationships with the adjective "loving." The fact of the matter is that most children around the world never have and never will experience a loving relationship with their human parents. I recently met a young man who is twenty-seven years old. His mother became pregnant and conceived him when she was fifteen years old. Frazzled, scared, and desperate, his mother threw him into a trash can behind his home. If it was not for his grandmother, who heard him crying, he would not be presently alive. His father? He spent twenty-five years in prison for murdering an undercover police officer. Their relationship is non-existent. Sin not only wreaked havoc on the family soon after the Fall, but it still does also today!

How do you find the strength to love your parents when they are so unloving? How do you even respect someone who either tried to discard you as a young baby or child? What are you to make of a murderous father? These are just a few examples of how alienation from God affects all human relationships. After the Fall of mankind, all human relationships became subject to sin's consequences. We were designed to enjoy our relationship with each other and God, not disdain it. This is one of the reasons why Christ's sacrifice on the cross is so crucial in relation to human familial relationships.

Fortunately, I was raised in a Christ-centered family. What I mean by "Christ-centered family" is that my parents both love Christ, and their love for Christ permeated all areas of our life as a family. It certainly doesn't mean our home was perfect, but Christ was the focus. My parents not only shared the gospel with me and my siblings, but they also lived it out before us. I thank the Lord often for their example of love. I am appreciative of all the efforts they made to ensure we grew up feeling loved and supported. But the greatest gift they have ever given me was Jesus. In fact, Christ is the greatest gift anyone can ever give their children.

I met with a young man once who was adopted by loving parents. By all accounts this young man is part of a loving, middle-class, hard-working, caring family. His non-biological parents love him deeply. They met with me asking for advice on how to handle his unbecoming behavior. Teenagers are prone toward rebellion. Couple that with a hormonal season of growth, you'll likely have an unruly child. Children struggle obeying their parents from the moment they are born. Human depravity is something we are born with. But if rebelliousness, disobedience, and insubordination were not part of God's original plan, what was his original intent?

First, let me address those of you who are parents. Parents are responsible for raising their children to hear the gospel, worship God, and function in society. Granted, every parent is tasked with raising sinful human beings into becoming decent and moral people.[49] This is an extremely difficult task since our children are born morally bankrupt. There's a tendency among postmodern people who live in a secularized society to think that we are inherently good. I reject this idea. All you have to do is look at a young child. It is harder to teach children to be good than how to be bad. My wife and I joke with friends that if you think people are born inherently good … you do not have children!

Raising children is more than simply making them responsible people one day. We belong to God, and this world is not our home. If we are to make an eternal impact in the lives of our children we must teach them that this world is not our ultimate destination. We need to share the gospel with them and pray for them to be transformed by its power. We must also live it. We need to show them how to live as aliens––as redeemed-foreigners––in this present world as ambassadors for the gospel

(1 Peter 1; 2 Corinthians 5).

According to the Westminster Confession of Faith, the chief goal of mankind is to glorify God and enjoy him forever. Your child will not have a full sense of purpose until he or she understands they were made for a divine purpose. Their passions, desires, and affections will likely be misplaced in earthly things if they do not understand life on earth is not all there is, if they do not understand we were created for worship.

Furthermore, in order for us to enjoy God forever, we must worship as an eternal endeavor. Home should be a place of worship. It should be a place where children experience the truths of the gospel. Only those who understand the way to eternal life is through repentance, forgiveness, and humility will enjoy God forever. Parents must teach gospel truth to their children and model a consistent life of worship.

Most parents wish they were experts in pediatric behavior. There are certainly many helpful resources like the Christian-based infant management book written by Gary Ezzo and pediatrician Robert Bucknam titled *On Becoming Baby Wise: Giving Your Infant the Gift of Nighttime Sleep*, Tedd Tripp's *Shepherding a Child's Heart*, and Amy McCready's *If I Have to Tell You One More Time*. Behavior modification has its place. But it must not be the ultimate goal for parenting.

Scripture helps guide our parenting. Loving God begins by teaching our children about what he means by that. Perhaps one of the most seminal passages in Scripture related to parenting is Deuteronomy 6:4–9 (notice the focus on parents, their children, and the life in the home),

Hear, O Israel: The Lord our God, the Lord is one. You shall

146

love the Lord your God with all your heart and with all your soul and with all your might. And these words that I command you today shall be on your heart. You shall teach them diligently to your children and shall talk of them when you sit in your house, and when you walk by the way, and when you lie down, and when you rise. You shall bind them as a sign on your hand, and they shall be as frontlets between your eyes. You shall write them on the doorposts of your house and on your gates.

Moses instructed the soon to be foreigners, the Israelites headed into the Promised Land, to fear the Lord and to teach their children to do the same. Such fear of God was to be propelled by love for God. Obeying one's parents is merely a training ground for obeying God himself. But parents must take the lead. Learning obedience is a rehearsal for our ultimate heavenly reality. Therefore, this reality should change our priorities and lives here on earth.

Here are a few things you can do as a parent to lead your child in both the fear and love of the Lord:

1. Pray and model a life of prayer with and before your children.
2. Read the Bible often to your children, even when (especially when) they are young.
3. Encourage and model honesty and vulnerability. Create space in your family for your children to confess their sins and their struggles. And for you to do the same.
4. Develop a regular family worship service time.
5. Teach them a biblically based Catechism. My wife and I use the New City Catechism.[50]
6. Attend church regularly and make sure your children are involved in a robust kids church program (i.e., Pre-

cepts, Awana, camps).

7. Serve locally in a Christian non-Profit, or globally through missionary engagement, and model sharing Christ.

Second, children need to know how to handle family dynamics. It is highly likely that if you are reading this book that you are an adult. I have lived long enough, and maybe you have also, to know that we all carry childhood baggage. I grew up under super loving, caring, godly parents. My mom taught us the Bible from a young age, my dad led us in prayer, worship, and modeled servant leadership. They have been married for 39 years. Sadly, that is not the norm.

One of the greatest challenges for children, as it relates to their earthly parents, is the issue of forgiveness. How do you forgive an abusive father, an overbearing mother, and the people who raised you under compulsion and even hatred? How do you obey your parents when they are not the best example of godly or good conduct? How do you honor your parents if they are disrespectful to you (Ephesians 6:1–2)? Alvin Reid writes,

> If you have been mistreated by others, God loves you and cares for you. He is not done with you. Reflect on how much He has forgiven you and ask His strength to forgive those who hurt you. Forgiving someone does not mean what they did wasn't real; it means you are no longer being defined by their actions but by God's grace.[51]

If you find yourself in this category, you are in the majority. The cure to your child/parent issues is forgiveness. Forgiveness is one of the marks of Christ followers. Paul encouraged believers to forgive. He wrote about what it means to be a new creation in Christ. In Ephesians 3, he reminds the church that we are "fellow heirs and fellows members of the body, and fellow partakers of Christ Jesus through the gospel." It is this same gospel that teaches us that we, who were alienated from God, have been granted a new identity. In the previous chapter he also reminded believers "are no longer strangers and aliens, but you are fellow citizens with the saints and members of the household of God" (Ephesians 2:19). Why does it matter? Because we are expected to live differently than the world.

Paul elaborates, "I therefore, a prisoner for the Lord, urge you to walk in a manner worthy of the calling to which you have been called, with all humility and gentleness, with patience, bearing with one another in love, eager to maintain the unity of the Spirit in the bond of peace" (Ephesians 4:1–3). He encouraged the church not to live as unredeemed foreigners, but rather as redeemed foreigners whose lives have been made new (Ephesians 4:20–24). Concluding the fourth chapter of Ephesians, he writes, "Be kind to one another, tenderhearted, forgiving one another, as God in Christ forgave you." We will never have to forgive someone for anything that compares with how much God forgave us through Jesus.

After his long explanation of what it means to be a Christ follower, Paul addresses the family. Children are called to obey their parents in the Lord. And by implication, children are also to forgive their parents as God in Christ forgave them. The ones closest to us are the hardest to forgive, including our parents. But if we are to live as redeemed-foreigners on earth, we must emulate our King who forgave us despite the fact he owed us nothing in return.

Here are some practical steps you can take in order to forgive your parents if they have failed you1.Pray for divinely given strength to forgive your father and/or mother.

> 1. Pray for divinely given strength to forgive your father and/or mother.
> 2. Seek godly counsel, have others pray with and for you.
>
> 3. Confide your struggle to forgive your parents with your spouse, friend, or a counselor.
>
> 4. Write a letter to your parents expressing your feelings, telling them about your hurt and pain, and tell them you forgive them for failing them. Not only will this be refreshing to you, but it will also help you collect your thoughts properly so you can "get everything off your chest." You will experience healing through the process.
>
> 5. Offer to meet with them, if they are able and willing, so you can speak to them about your heartaches and express your words of forgiveness.

Family Dynamics

God loves the family. The heavenly worship gathering of the saints will be composed of fathers, mothers, husbands, wives, brothers, and sisters. The Scripture clearly points to the remaking of the family. The day of the Lord will come. Though most families are broken, and all families are composed of broken people, there will be a day when God will make all things well for those who believe in him. He will restore the family. We will be part of a heavenly family sustained by a perfect Father. In the meantime, we have the opportunity to point others to Christ. We can model what it means to be part of our heavenly family in practical ways. Here are two main ways our families can live as redeemed-foreigners pointing others to Christ, one to avoid and one to affirm: 1) a denial of materialism, 2) practicing hospitality.

First, materialism teaches us to love earthly things more than they are worth. Do you think anyone in heaven will miss earth when we get there? My guess is, absolutely not! So, why do we focus on earthly things so much? If we are to point others to a heavenly destination, we must deny all earthly attractions. Earthly things distract us because we are idolatrous and materialistic. Materialism is one of the most prominent idols in the western world. However, the temptation toward earthly things is nothing new.

Christ warned his disciples not to lay up for themselves treasures on earth. He was referring to material things that can be destroyed by moth and rust. Things that can also be stolen by thieves. I can relate to the latter since my parents' home has been broken into multiple times. The alternative? to lay up for ourselves treasures in heaven. In other words, to be more preoccupied with eternal things rather than earthly things that fade (Matthew 6:19–21).

This short-sighted type of thinking materialism produces is detrimental not only to us, but to our witness. If God is our Lord, we must serve him only (Matthew 6:24). We must be reminded that we are in the world but are not of the world (John 17). And the best place to start is within our own families.

The goal of our life is not to accumulate as many earthly possessions as we possibly can. Steve Jobs was not able to take

once single penny with him when he died. Our material possessions are irrelevant if not used for kingdom purposes. That is
why Jesus urged his disciples to lay treasures in heaven. Even the
fanciest car, home, or boat on earth rusts and decays. But we fool
ourselves into thinking material things can bring us purpose.
Materialism preaches self-sufficiency, arrogance, and covetousness. None of these are elements of purpose.

Our primary goal as parents is not to raise our children to
be successful, but rather to point them to salvation. That is why
we must fight against materialism. Our goal is to point them
to find their full satisfaction in Christ alone, for nothing in the
world can offer us is able to bring us significance. Albert Barnes
is right to say, "Our earthly possessions will indeed perish in
the final wreck of all things; but let the ship perish, let all we
have sink in the deep, if we may come 'safe to land.' From these
storms and billows––these dangerous seas––these tempestuous
voyages–––may we all be brought at last safe to heaven."[52]

Second, home is the primary place for Christians to practice hospitality. Most cultures around the world practice hospitality through sharing food, providing lodging, and home
gatherings. In ancient cultures strangers were welcomed in
one's home when passing through a city. The home "was a
place where biblical hospitality could be practiced and demon-
strated—a sign of authentic fellowship among Christians that
also served as a collective witness to non-believing guests."[53]
Sam Chan provides great insight on the benefits of hospitality,

> Hospitality is costly. It costs time, effort, and money. It's
> a form of generosity. But hospitality gives a social capital.
> It allows us to earn our friends trust so we can talk about
> things that matter. And if we've been generous to them,

then they will most likely reciprocate by listening to our views, even if they don't agree with what we're saying. Hospitality also makes the house *vulnerable* – we're opening up our private homes to our guess. But in doing so, hospitality invites the guests to be vulnerable in return. This is a safe space where they can talk about private matters that are weighing on their hearts.[54]

I remember when I came to America having the feeling of being completely out of place. Encountering a new culture, customs, and worldviews was overwhelming. But it was through the hospitality of my college friends, other redeemed-foreigners, and folks who appreciated me, that I was able to overcome difficult cultural barriers. My friends would host me in their home during school breaks. My Spring, Fall, and Christmas breaks were spent in other people's homes. I grew to love each family that showed me hospitality. I was so blessed by their kindness!

Today, fast forward almost two decades, Ashli and I host folks at our home. In the past nine years of our marriage, we have had multiple people living with us. We decided to open our home to others early on in our relationship. We believe our home is the Lord's. Does not everything belong to God? Having this type of mentality is crucial for families seeking to be a blessing to others through hospitality. I have met many American couples and families who live in huge homes but have never experienced the joy of hospitality. They are missing out!

The Bible tells us to show hospitality to others, especially strangers (foreigners). Romans 12:13 says, "Contribute to the needs of the saints and seek to show hospitality." The word hospitality is connected with the word "practice." It has the idea of "being given to" something. In other words, we should seek to continuously practice hospitality. Hebrews 13:2a also reminds us, "Let brotherly love continue. Do not neglect to show hospitality to strangers [foreigners]."

Interestingly enough, the word hospitality, both in the book of Romans and Hebrews, is the word *philoxenia*. It means to love strangers. The Greek *xenia* is a derivative of *xenos*, mentioned above in a discussion about xenophobia. The message is simple. Instead of being afraid of strangers and foreigners, we ought to love them.

We need to seek to show hospitality to others. Hospitality is usually fueled by generosity. Being generous teaches you to detach yourself from worldly things. We must ask ourselves if we hold on to things with an open hand or a closed fist? One of the true marks of a redeemed-foreigner is generosity through hospitality. How generous are you with your earthly possessions and resources? God is generous. One day you'll enjoy your heavenly inheritance from the Lord as a heavenly-citizen, why not share what you already have with others now?

The Heavenly-Minded Family

The false promise of materialism is a life of comfort. Materialism lures us into thinking that suffering can be overcome via attaching ourselves to earthly things. Therefore, parents work hard to provide comfort for their children. Parents work multiple jobs not only to make ends meet, but to provide the best of the best for their family. Meanwhile, familial relationships decay. Children live with absent fathers and mothers who are physically present, but never attentive. Spouses lose intimacy because they are stressed, tired, and worn out from their jobs.

I am not minimizing the fact that many of us do have to work multiple jobs to feed our family. What I am referring to is the ugly side of our earthly pursuit of comfort. If many of us were to examine our earthly priorities, we would have to admit that often our earthly pursuits have zero to no eternal value. But we must seek to balance our earthly pursuits with heavenly priorities. Why is it important to hold our lives in balance when it comes to earthly living? It is important, because whatever this world has to offer us is finite. It is broken and limited. It cannot be sustained for long. That is why Jesus used the analogy of moth and rust, calling us to give ourselves to eternal things rather than things that fade away (Matthew 6:19–21).

Our earthly living is also important, because our goal in life is to honor and glorify God, knowing that this world is not our home. So, whether we have little or much, we can still be content. Paul talked about how he had learned to be content in times of feast or famine (Philippians 4:10-13). Paul knew God supplies for our needs "according to His riches in glory in Christ Jesus" (Philippians 4:19). He was content and heavenly focused.

Can you say that your family lives in contentment and is heavenly focused?

This question is not meant to evoke doubt or fear. Rather, it should help us to reflect on whether or not our lives are too earthly minded versus heavenly focused. Contentment does not equal comfort. Because one can be content whether or not he is living comfortably. Contentment is rooted in the promises of God. It is rooted in knowing that as redeemed-foreigners we will one day have everything we need and much more when we reach our heavenly destination.

When we understand that heaven is our home, our earthly mindset changes. We can say with Paul, "For me to live is Christ, and to die is gain." We can also face our trials and tribulations with confidence. No matter what anyone in our family is going through. Whether we experience loss of property, job loss, or even loss of life. As Paul so eloquently puts it,

> So, we do not lose heart. Though our outer self is wasting away, our inner self is being renewed day by day. For this light momentary affliction is preparing for us an eternal weight of glory beyond all comparison, as we look not to the things that are seen but to the things that are unseen. For the things that are seen are transient, but the things that are unseen are eternal (2 Corinthians 4:16–18)

We can be content as we look forward to spending eternity in the presence of our Lord as heavenly citizens. A heavenly-minded family understands that suffering is only a tool for our sanctification. We can suffer and have joy, because we know this world is not our home. Having a heavenly-minded attitude also helps us to understand that the comforts of this world are transient. Whether or not we suffer on earth, we are secure in Christ. Nothing can ever separate us from his love (Romans 8:38–39). Our families will remain strong and can face the storms of life when we develop a heaven-toward mentality.

CHAPTER NINE

Society

You have nothing to do but to save souls. Therefore, spend and be spent in this work. And go not only to those that need you, but to those that need you most. It is not your business to preach so many times, and to take care of this or that society; but to save as many souls as you can; to bring as many sinners as you possibly can to repentance –
John Wesley

G uess What? I believe John Wesley is right! The church of Jesus Christ exists to impact the world with the gospel message for the glory of God. The world craves for hope as it decays. The church has limited resources, but it is also empowered by the Holy Spirit to be a witness to the world. The task of missions will continue to be difficult. However, the Lord commanded his church to go into the world to make disciples. The church becomes light to the world as it proclaims the gospel with boldness to the lost and ministers to people's needs in their own context. It is important to note that Wesley also engaged in benevolent ministries, education, and was very influential in the abolition of slavery in Great Britain.

We were tasked with the proclamation of the gospel to all humanity, all societies, at all times until Christ returns. Society changes, cultures change, and people change, but the gospel message remains.

Growing up I participated in a lot of social work. I was part of an orphanage ministry, prison ministry, went on mission trips, and helped at food banks. I have several friends who lived in poverty as their parents struggled to make ends meet. Not to mention seeing homeless children begging for food on the streets of my hometown on a regular basis, and seeing entire neighborhoods ravished with impoverishment.

All societies are broken. In other words, they are affected by sin. It is the consequence of the Fall. One day, God will establish a perfect society in the new city of Jerusalem. But that day is still to come. None of our earthly societies are ever going to function perfectly. So, what are Christians to do in relation to earthly societies? Are we to seek to reform them? Are we the primary agents of change to society? Yes and No. Let me explain.

Christians As Society Influencers – Yes

Yes, Christians are called to influence the societies in which they live. As foreigners, we influence societies in the way we live for God as redeemed-foreigners. In the Old Testament, the precedent was set as God encouraged his exiled people to "seek the peace of the city" God sent them to (Jeremiah 29:7). In the New Testament, Christians are told to submit to governmental powers and even pray for them (Romans 13:1–7; Titus 3:1; 1 Peter 2:13–17). But keep in mind, that much of New Testament teaching warns Christians not to be corrupted by the world (John 17:15–18; 1 Corinthians 5:9–10; Romans 12:2; James 4:4).

Christians are known for their influence in society. Christians have long held views against abortion. In fact, most pro-life groups are Christian. Christians have also long held that the family nucleus should be preserved. The biblical view of marriage between one man and one woman is the biblical model for the family. Therefore, for instance, Christians seek to champion ideas that are contrary to secularized societies. Secularism preaches freedom of expression, but its basis of morality is not found in God. Rather, the individual is free to choose as he/she wishes. Christians, instead, base their morality on the person and character of God as revealed in Scripture. That is why Christians have sought to make a tangible impact on society when it comes to moral issues.

Christians have a long track history of charitable work. Alvin J. Schmidt makes the case that Christians have made a substantial impact on societies in his book *How Christianity Changed the World*. Christians have worked to help women, slaves, labor workers, the unborn and young, orphans, widows, and the marginalized be treated with the proper respect they deserve, because they were created in the image of God. Our quest is fueled by Christ himself. Schmidt points out that Jesus changed not only individual lives, but civilizations. He writes, "In the ancient world, his teachings elevated brutish standards of morality, halted infanticide, enhanced human life, emancipated women, abolished slavery, inspired charities and relief organizations, created hospitals, established orphanages, and founded schools."[55]

The greatest and most prominent universities of today were originally founded for "Christian" purposes. Much of science was influenced by Christians. Though many criticize Christianity, the leading scientific figures of the sixteenth and seventeenth centuries were Christians. Christianity's history is not without fault, but its impact on societies, even to this day, is undeniable.

Christians As Society Influencers – No

Do not get me wrong. I am not saying that Christians should avoid making an impact in society. Christ ministered to the poor, engaged the marginalized, and fed the hungry. Jesus argued with the intellectuals of his day about such issues. Further, the light of the gospel is the only hope for a world that praises the wicked, elevates immorality, and encourages morality as "anything goes" without regard for others. There are certain aspects of culture that are to be appreciated, and sometimes even celebrated. However, as redeemed-foreigners, the line between witness and compromise is often thin.

Jesus, the ultimate foreigner, became the primary example of what it means to be *in* the world, but not *of* the world. To the scribes and Pharisees, he said, "You are of this world; I am not of this world" (John 8:23). His conviction came from the understanding that this world is not our home. Jesus said, "My kingdom is not of this world. If it were, my servants would fight to prevent my arrest by the Jewish leaders. But now my kingdom is from another place." Jesus understood his focus on earth was eternal, and so should we.

So, how should redeemed-foreigners engage with society? Should we not seek to stand against abortion? Poverty? Injustices? Racism? And engage in human rights efforts? The answer is, of course we should. However, our primary focus should be to offer the world an otherworldly solution to all these problems, namely Jesus. We must offer the world a hope that is beyond earthly things. But we have to "walk and chew gum at the same time." We must offer non-redeemed foreigners the hope of the gospel while we take action against the evils of this world. We must also understand we cannot cure the world. Only God can. We need to be both sober and conscious of the fact that our actions toward social justice will never be enough to eternally change all that is wrong with the world.

Today, a lot of redeemed-foreigners are more concerned with social action than gospel proclamation. I recently heard the testimony of a woman who volunteers at a non-profit Christian ministry. When asked why she was involved in helping the marginalized, she said, "There is just a warm feeling you feel in your heart when you help folks." There was no mention of Jesus, the gospel, or the redemption God offers those who are lost. One can conclude, even though I am not fully ascribing motive, that she was engaging in this local ministry simply because it made her feel good.

Kevin DeYoung and Greg Gilbert provide great insight as it relates to Christian social action. They write, "It is not the church's responsibility to right every wrong or to meet every need, though we have biblical motivation to do some of both. It is our responsibility, however—our unique mission and plain priority—that this unpopular, impractical gospel message gets told, that neighbors and nations may know that Jesus is the Christ, the Son of God, and that by believing, they may have life in his name."[56]

The same is true of political action. Pastor John Piper offers some great insight from an interview with one of his radio listeners. His listener asked, "Obviously, as Christians, we are to live as strangers, exiles, aliens, and pilgrims on this earth. Is there an appropriate place in the Christian life to be patriotic? If so, what is it? And at what point does our patriotism go too far?" To which Piper responded, "Yes, I think there is [room for patriotism] and I think it's right, or at least it can be right and good." But "it is true that we need to stress it at the beginning, maybe stress it at the end, we are pilgrims here, we are exiles, refugees, sojourners ... In the end, Christ has relativized all human allegiances, all human loves. Keeping Christ supreme in our affections makes all our lesser loves better, not worse."[57] In other words, rather than elevating earthly patriotism, we should elevate kingdom allegiance. We should point others to the greater reality of the perfect heavenly kingdom of Christ to which all are invited to partake.

The point? As redeemed-foreigners we seek to change the world in Christ's name for the glory of God through our actions. The Bible tells us we ought to. James writes, "Religion that is pure and undefiled before God the Father is this: to visit orphans and widows in their affliction, and to keep oneself unstained from the world" (James 1:27). But we must understand our actions here are both temporary and limited. Furthermore, we cannot forget that our actions toward the marginalized are just as important as keeping ourselves "unstained from the world." The solution is to be both a hearer and a doer of the Word.

So how should we engage with society? By being a light in the world (Matthew 5:14–16), while at the same time understanding the sober reality that our earthly actions are always going to be limited. DeYoung and Gilbert observe, "It seems to us a better, and more realistic way to think about the world in this present age is to realize that until Jesus comes back, we will (as he told us, in fact) 'always have the poor' with us (Matthew 26:11), and that our societies and civilizations will always be marked by corruption, injustice, and even oppression."[58] They add, "We should fight against and resist the evil in the world with a square-shouldered realization that God does not expect us to be able to make the world perfect, and that those evils will persist until our King comes back to end them."

The goal of Christian social action must be God's glory. Afterall, that is the goal of all Christian service. We must both live out our faith and meet the needs of others (James 2:14–18). We must seek to combine Christian social action with Christ-centered gospel proclamation. Further, we must show the world this world is not our home. The best is yet to come. One day those who inherited the kingdom will no longer suffer, and all injustices will cease to exist because God will make all things right again.

Heavenly-Minded Influencers

Heavenly-minded influencers are driven by a desire to glorify God with the time and resources they have been given while on earth. The way to rid ourselves of materialism and earthly-minded thinking is to set our minds on heavenly matters (Colossians 3:1–4). Having this type of mentality produces the fuel that helps us fight our earthly desires like sexual immorality, untoward passions, impurity, evil desires, and covetousness (Philippians 3:5). On the flip side, as redeemed-foreigners––or as Paul puts it "God's chosen ones" who are holy and beloved––we replace these earthly sinful desires with compassionate hearts, humility, meekness, patience, forgiveness and genuine love (Philippians 3:12–14).

Social Media has created a new category for social interaction. Prior to the ascension of social media platforms and technology, people were only able to relate on a regular basis with people in their close inner circles. Today, through the power of technology, people are able to influence others across the globe through marketing, branding, information, and much more. Human social interaction has taken a whole new form as people engage in conversations with others virtually more than in person.

Have you ever heard the term "influencer"? At the most basic level, Merriam-Webster defines an influencer as, "one who exerts influence: a person who inspires or guides the actions of others."[59] There are many types of influencers. The most commonly known are the social media influencers. Social media influencers include bloggers, YouTubers, celebrities, and other entrepreneurial people that have established at least one million online followers. Most people, myself included, are not ever going to come close to having that many online followers. However, each of us can influence others for the glory of God.

God has given us different platforms to disseminate his gospel message. As redeemed-foreigners, we have the greatest message the world has ever heard. And today, we can influence others without even physically leaving our home. My friend Jeff is an example. Jeff is passionate about sharing the Gospel with others. A few years ago, he met a young man online who lives in Pakistan. This young man desired to become a pastor. Their connection? The internet.

Jeff began mentoring the young man via online Bible studies. Soon, others began to join their Bible study. A small congregation was formed. Now people have come to faith in Jesus Christ, and several have been baptized. What started as an internet interaction turned into a small church in Pakistan, led by a young pastor who loves Jesus and is tangibly changing his own society. Through the years both Jeff and this young man have walked through loss and pain together, even though they live across the globe from each other, and they have also experienced the goodness and sweetness of the Lord through their relationship and influence.

Did you know that God has placed you exactly where you are for a reason? Did you know your time and location are divinely predetermined? In Acts 17:26–27, the apostle Paul writes, "And he made from one man every nation of mankind to live on all the face of the earth, having determined allotted periods and the boundaries of their dwelling place, that they should seek God, and perhaps feel their way toward him and find him. Yet he is actually not far from each one of us." Note the reason why God has placed each of us where we are, so that we should seek God, and perhaps feel our way toward him and find him.

God has placed you where you are for an eternal purpose. If you have already been found by him, then you have a purpose to fulfill: to bring him glory in all that you do and wherever you go. As redeemed-foreigners, we honor God by offering up our time, talents, and treasure so that others may also find him. My friend Steve is an example. Steve has been in the real estate business for decades. After succeeding and doing well, he decided to use his business for missional purposes. Instead of hoarding his profit from real estate earnings, Steve decided to give money away to different ministries around the world.

Steve uses his real estate skills to invest in new properties. As properties are bought and sold, the remaining profit is given to various ministries. In the past 4 years, his organization has given over $300,000 to ministries in Brazil, India, Romania, Ukraine, the Democratic Republic of Congo, Pakistan, and Haiti. His organization, through personal business, has impacted the lives of thousands of people around the globe. Why? Because Steve has understood his time, treasure, and talent can influence others to know Christ in tangible ways.

They seek to leave a footprint of gospel influence in the world for the glory of God. BAM Global is the primary example of this model. Their vision is to become "A movement of businesses transforming people and nations – for God's glory!"[60] They do so by developing a "biblically sound and practical understanding of business." Their desired outcome is aligned with what it means to live as redeemed-foreigners awaiting heavenly citizenship,

> The group defined its purpose as identifying principles, models and practices of business that give expression to its role in advancing God's purpose or mission in the world. The group operated on the basis that, broadly speaking, God's purpose is to establish His Kingdom— a Kingdom to be fully consummated with the second coming of Jesus Christ but inaugurated in 'this present age' (Titus 2:11–14).[61]

The idea of using one's business for missions is biblical. BAM global created a wealth creation manifesto that clarifies the biblical impetus for using business as mission. Through the creation of wealth, not in the sense of the prosperity gospel, lives and societies are indeed transformed:

1. God is Creator of all things: Gen 1:1-2:4; Neh 9:6; Ps 104; Rev 4:11

2. Earth belongs to God: Lev 25:23; 1 Chron 29:11; Ps 24:1; 1 Cor 10:26; Gen 2:15

3. God is the giver of wealth: 1 Chron 29:11-12; Prov 8:18-21

4. Our creation in God's image: Gen 1:26,27; Gen 9:6

5. Our work as people made in God's image: Gen 1:26,28; Gen 2:15; Eph 4:8; 1 Tim 5:8

6. The command to work (and rest): Gen 2:15; Ex 20:9-11; Deut 5:13-15

7. Bezalel and craftsmen for tabernacle enabled by God: Ex 36:1-2

8. Wealth creation is both a gift from God and a command: Deut 8:11-18; Deut 28:11,12; Eccl 5:19

9. Hard work leads to wealth: Prov 10:4; Prov 13:4; Prov 18:9 (condemnation of idleness); Prov 20:13

10. All useful work is to be done to God's glory: Col 3:23,24

11. Wise investors are commended: Matt 25:16-30; Luke 19:11-27

12. Examples of "righteous rich" include Abraham (Gen 13:2), Isaac (Gen 26:12,13), Boaz (Ruth 2), David (1 Chron 28-29), David's supporters while he was in exile, esp. Barzillai, 'a very rich man' (2 Sam 17:27-29, 19:32); Solomon (1 Kgs 3:9-14), Nehemiah (Neh 5), Job (Job 1,29,31,42)

13. Markers of a functioning and restored marketplace: Jer 32

14. A businesswoman, Lydia, who furthers the gospel: Acts 16:14-15

15. Call to equip God's people for service: Eph 4:11-16

16. Call to witness and make disciples in all nations: Matt 28:18-20; Acts 1:8

17. Perils of hoarding: Prov 11:26; Luke 12:16-21; James 5:3

18. Encouragement to sharing: Acts 2:44-45; Acts 4:32; 2 Cor 8:1-15; 2 Cor 9:6-15; 1 Tim 6:18; Heb 13:16

19. Call to generosity: Deut 15:10; Ps 37:21,26; Ps 112:5; Prov 11:25; 2 Cor 9:6;1 Tim 6:18; Acts 20:35

20. Virtue of contentment: Phil 4:11-12; 1 Tim 6:6,8; Heb 13:5

21. Examples of different choices of how to handle wealth: Job 29:1-25; Luke 19:1-10; Acts 4:32-5:11; love of wealth does not satisfy (Eccl 5:10)

22. Calls to help the poor: Ex 23:11; Lev 19:10; Deut 15:7-11; Prov 19:17; Prov 28:27; Prov 31:20; Matt 19:21

23. Extrapolating from the microcosm of the family: how the noble woman's business ventures create wealth for her family: Prov 31:10-21

24. Israel's wealth increased because God gave them the 'ability to produce wealth': Deut 8:7-18 – through productive agricultural work, through trade/selling & buying, and through mining; also, through obedience (Deut 28:1,11-12; 2 Chron 26:4-5)

25. God's blessing on nations through material prosperity: Deut 30:9

26. God's blessing of material prosperity through pursuit of wisdom: Prov 3:16

27. The call to justice: Ps 106:3; Prov 29:7; Is 1:17; Amos 5:24; Zech 7:9, Micah 6:8

28. Sensitivity to context: 1 Cor 9:19-23

29. Power of trade to create wealth (and to corrupt the wealthy): Ezek 27-28 (ch 27:12-24 is the most complete and extensive list of trading communities in the Bible)

30. Dependency on agricultural production (equivalent of business in contemporary times): Eccl 5:9; King Uzziah understood this, see 2 Chron 26:10

31. Wealthy Christians in the early church known for generosity in helping the poor and/or building the church: Joseph called Barnabas (Acts 4:36-37); Dorcas (Acts 9:36); Cornelius (Acts 10:1); Lydia (Acts 16:13-15, 40); Jason

(Acts 17:5-9); Aquila and Priscilla (Acts 18:2-3); Mnason of Cyprus (Acts 21:16); Phoebe (Rom 16:1); Erastus (Rom 16:23); Chloe (1 Cor 1:11).

Being a heavenly-minded influencer means that we use our earthly resources to the best of our abilities for the glory of God. We can use our business, job, social media platforms, or leadership skills in creative ways to advance the message of the gospel to a lost world. We can help others find God and be transformed into redeemed-foreigners. You too can be a heavenly-minded influencer.

CHAPTER TEN

Church

"Each generation of the church in each setting has the responsibility of communicating the gospel in understandable terms, considering the language and thought-forms of that setting" – Francis Shaeffer

"The church is not the way to heaven; the church is the sign that points to heaven" – Adrian Rogers

Guess What? The church is God's plan to proclaim the message of the gospel to non-redeemed foreigners. God has chosen you and I to take part in his mission. Growing up, I thought it was my pastor's job to preach God's Word to others. But now I understand we are all preachers, just with different platforms. Preaching means proclamation. Proclamation can take place behind a pulpit, or anywhere any of us proclaim the good news of Jesus Christ.

The church is God's Plan A for the world. Pastor David Platt puts it this way,

We are the plan of God, and there is no plan B. Of course, God has the power to write the gospel in letters across the clouds so that people can learn about Jesus and believe in him. But in his infinite wisdom, he has not chosen this route. Instead, he has chosen to use us as ambassadors who carry the gospel to people who have never heard the name of Jesus.[62]

Note that Platt uses the term "ambassadors" in reference to God's plan in choosing the church to carry the gospel message forth. He is right! The challenge, however, is that the church can be easily lured in compromising its mission and calling. Historically, the church has struggled not to identify itself with the world while living in the world.

The church is God's agent in a fallen and broken world. As previously mentioned, the church, which is the community of redeemed-foreigners, is in the world, but called to be not of the world. Paul urged the church not to be "conformed" into the pattern of this world (Romans 12:2). The word connotes the idea of avoiding being molded into someone else's patterns, both in mind and character.[63] The Bible warns the church not to be enamored with the world, in Jesus' own words,

> Do not love the world or the things in the world. If anyone loves the world, the love of the Father is not in him. For all that is in the world—the desires of the flesh and the desires of the eyes and pride of life—is not from the Father but is from the world. And the world is passing away along with its desires, but whoever does the will of God abides forever (1 John 2:15–17).

The NTL puts it this way, "For the world offers only a craving for physical pleasure, a craving for everything we see, and pride in our achievements and possessions." Why is this important for us to fight against? Because it matters to God. Friendship with the world is enmity with God (James 4:4). The church not only is to remain unstained by the world; it must also carry on God's mission.

The Mission Of The Church

The mission of the church is to proclaim the gospel message to non-redeemed foreigners for the glory of God. As redeemed-foreigners we are commanded to make disciples of all nations in the name of the Father, Son, and Holy Spirit. The mission of the church must be understood in light of God's mission, the *missio Dei*. The church exists to partner with God's desire to see his name glorified and his kingdom proclaimed. The *missio Dei* is about God. The church nearly participates in his agenda for the world. Keith Whitfield argues, "God's mission is to make himself known to his creation and that this is the driving plan for God's purposes for all of history."[64]

God's desire was for his chosen people, who believe in him by faith, to become his ambassadors on earth (2 Corinthians 5:20; Ephesians 6:20; 1 Peter 2:9). His faithful ones were given the task (mission) to proclaim the king, his kingdom (domain), and his message (the gospel). The church does not advance the kingdom, but rather it proclaims its message. Piper puts it this way, "Missions is not the ultimate goal of the church. Worship is. Missions exists because worship doesn't. Worship is ultimate, not missions, because God is ultimate, not man."[65] We proclaim the gospel for the praise of His glory.

The church is a visible representation of the kingdom's presence on the earth. Doug Coleman writes, "The church does not continue the kingdom, but it is 'the concrete display of the already/not yet' of the Kingdom. Therefore, the church is currently the primary means through which God is accomplishing his mission."[66] Jesus told his disciples, "As the Father sent me, I send you (John 20:21)." This "sending" is nothing less than a mission. A mission that aims to proclaim salvation to those who are condemned to eternal hell.[67] Andreas Köstenberger and Peter O'Brien are correct in believing that "the saving mission of Jesus constitutes the foundation for Christian mission, and the Christian gospel is the message of mission, a mission that is not optional but mandatory."[68] The church is sent into the world as a missional agent for the proclamation of the gospel.

In a certain sense the church does not "have" a mission. The church is not missional because of its mission activity. Jürgen Moltmann puts it this way, "What we have to learn from them is not that the church 'has' a mission, but the very reverse: that the mission of Christ creates its own church. Mission does not come from the church; it is from mission and in the light of mission that the church has to be understood."[69] The church's missional activity is related to its own identity. Michael Goheen points out that, "At its best, 'missional' describes not a specific activity of the church but the very essence and identity of the church as it takes up its role in God's story in the context of its culture and participates in God's mission to the world."[70] He further clarifies, "Thus, to describe the church as 'missional' is to define the entire Christian community as a body sent to the world and existing not for itself but to bring good news to the world."[71]

The Great Commission gives the followers of Jesus the task to make disciples of all nations (Matthew 28:18–20). The eschatological (end time) function of the church is to proclaim the gospel in the whole world. Christ said to his disciples, "And this gospel of the kingdom will be preached in the whole world as a testimony to all nations, and then the end will come" (Matthew 24:14). This task is still not completed.

Today, according to the Joshua Project, there are 17,433 people groups on planet earth. 7,407 are still unreached.[72] The earth's population currently has 7.6 billion people, which means 3,23 billion are still unreached. Unreached people groups are given this designation because something is happening in such people groups of the world, but not yet enough to see their whole people hear the gospel. In other words, there are over 3 billion foreigners who have not yet been given the message of redemption. They will remain non-redeemed foreigners if someone does not take the gospel to them.

Paul clearly communicated that the message of the gospel is salvation to everyone who believes. Those who confess Jesus with their mouth through repentance upon hearing the gospel are saved. But how can people be saved if they have not yet heard the gospel message? That is why he writes,

> How then will they call on him in whom they have not believed? And how are they to believe in him of whom they have never heard? And how are they to hear without someone preaching? And how are they to preach unless they are sent? As it is written, "How beautiful are the feet of those who preach the good news!" (Romans 10:14–15)

If you are wondering how they will hear it, there is only one way. God's people need to proclaim it! And perhaps the Lord may call you to share your faith among unreached people groups for his glory. Will you heed His call to go if he calls you?

The Marks Of The Church

Local congregations are visible representations of God's kingdom on earth. As a group of redeemed-foreigners, the church seeks not only to influence the world with the gospel, but also to teach it and apply it. In order to effectively carry out the gospel mandate churches must be healthy. A healthy church is a Christocentric church. But this Christocentricity needs to be filtered through its ecclesiology, or church functions. Mark Dever and some of his colleagues identify 9 marks of a healthy church: 1) preaching, 2) biblical theology, 3) the gospel, 4) conversion, 5) evangelism, 6) membership, 7) discipline, 8) discipleship, and 9) leadership.[73]

In the remainder of this final chapter, I will explore three of these nine marks, and offer one more.

Discipleship

As the good news of the gospel is proclaimed to non-redeemed foreigners, the church must also seek to grow disciples into maturity. That is why discipleship is so foundational for the health of the body of Christ. As Christianity is challenged by the winds of post-modernism and secularism, other world religions, and worldviews, the church must seek to find ways to properly disciple new believers. As new believers enter the kingdom, the church is tasked with the role of instructing them on how to participate in the mission of God. Without an understanding of how biblical revelation fits together believers are left ill-equipped to share the gospel.

Discipleship is the work of the church in equipping the

saints to grow in the knowledge of Christ. We should spur one another to love and good works (Heb 10:24). We help each other grow in Christ. 2 Peter 3:18 says, "But grow in the grace and knowledge of our Lord and Savior Jesus Christ. To him be glory both now and forever! Amen." As we help each other grow in Christ our maturity level increases. Paul says in Ephesians 4:15, "Rather, speaking the truth in love, we are to grow up in every way into him who is the head, into Christ."

It is important to note that the word "discipleship" does not appear in Scripture. The word "disciple" does. The Greek *mathētēs* evokes the idea of someone who is a learner or a pupil. Jesus chose twelve disciples. He invested in them and taught them what it means to be heavenly-minded and focused. He exemplified godly living before them. He walked with them, ate, laughed, and shared his wisdom with them so they would mature in godliness.

Before he ascended into heaven Jesus commanded his disciples (*mathētēs*) to make disciples (*mathēteuō*). They were to proclaim the gospel to others (foreigners) in order to lead them into conversion (redeemed foreigners), and then after baptizing them, they were to teach new disciples what it means to be kingdom representatives and ambassadors. Jesus' main message was about the kingdom of God. Redeemed-foreigners who will one day enjoy full heavenly citizenship can live out kingdom values on earth. In fact, it is through living out kingdom values that others recognize we are not of this world (John 13:35).

When Jesus told his disciples to baptize new converts in the name of the triune God, he also told them to teach them everything he taught them, adding the promise that he would be with them until the end of the age (Matthew 28:20). The word "teaching" in Matthew 28:20 is an active particle verb. In other words, it is a verb that connotes ongoing action. Discipleship involves active participation. And this participation is coupled with the Word of God.

The words "all that I have commanded you" in Matthew 28:20 refer to Scripture. Why is Scripture so important for discipleship? Paul gives us the answer, "All Scripture is breathed out by God and profitable for teaching, for reproof, for correction, and for training in righteousness, that the man of God may be complete, equipped for every good work" (2 Timothy 3:16). Not only is God's word inspired, but it is also the means by which, through discipleship, we are complete and equipped to do God's work.

In his letter to Titus Paul urged older men and women to teach the younger generation. His words have a profound impact for our understanding of discipleship within the context of the local church,

> Older men are to be sober-minded, dignified, self-controlled, sound in faith, in love, and in steadfastness. Older women likewise are to be reverent in behavior, not slanderers or slaves to much wine. They are to teach what is good, and so train the young women to love their husbands and children, to be self-controlled, pure, working at home, kind, and submissive to their own husbands, so that the word of God may not be reviled (Titus 2:2–5).

The emphasis is placed at the end with the words, "so that the word of God may not be reviled." Further, younger men were encouraged to "adorn the doctrine of God our Savior" (Titus 2:10). The word "doctrine" in Titus, is from the same root of the word "teaching" in Matthew 28:20.

Paul summarizes the reason why discipleship is so important in the same chapter as he concludes,

> For the grace of God has appeared, bringing salvation for all people, training us to renounce ungodliness and worldly passions, and to live self-controlled, upright, and godly lives in the present age, waiting for our blessed hope, the appearing of the glory of our great God and Savior Jesus Christ, who gave himself for us to redeem us from all lawlessness and to purify for himself a people for his own possession who are zealous for good works (Titus 2:11–14).

First, Paul points out that those who have been brought to salvation need to be trained to renounce ungodliness and worldly passions. Redeemed-foreigners must seek to live a life free from this world's passions. Second, redeemed-foreigners are marked by a life of self-control, uprightness, and godliness "in the present age." In other words, believers must conform their lives to godliness on earth. Why? Because, as Paul finally points out, those who have been saved wait for a future time when our heavenly citizenship will be realized. Christ will appear in a future time and take his redeemed-foreigners into glory.

Evangelism

Can we affect culture with the gospel? Some people may answer such a question in the positive, some with a more pessimistic disposition. Cultures are indeed complex. Regardless of one's view, the church engages culture in order to shape it through the lens of the gospel. Harvey M. Conn places missions and culture in perspective, "The goal of missions must be larger, to bring our cultures into conformity to the Kingdom of God and its fullness. The whole of cultural life ought to be subjected to the royal authority of him who has redeemed us by his blood (Matthew 28:18–20)."[74] As previously mentioned, the most eternally worthwhile way to impact our world is through gospel proclamation, not simply through social action and charity alone.

Local churches have often neglected evangelism. Most Christians are taught that evangelistic engagement equals inviting someone to attend a church worship service. This approach places the responsibility of gospel proclamation upon the church clergy rather than the believer. Another popular approach is to simply serve people. Whether a believer serves in a church parking lot ministry, as a volunteer in children's ministry, as a deacon, or in any particular ministry within a local congregation, the idea is to simply render service to others.

In recent times, a popular phrase, which is falsely attributed to St. Francis, reads, "Preach the gospel, and when necessary use words." Many who use this phrase that others can come to faith simply by one's good works, without the use of words. But this idea is completely contradictory to Scripture. The reason? Paul explains, "So faith comes from hearing, and hearing through the word of Christ" (Romans 10:17). In the same chapter Paul asks, "How then will they call on Him in whom they have not believed? How will they believe in Him whom they have not *heard*? And how will they *hear* without a preacher?" The emphasis is on hearing, not serving others. Serving is good, but our evangelistic efforts must be accompanied by the heralding of God's word. In other words, we must preach the gospel always, and use words. That said, the New Testament also teaches us to live lives that reflect the gospel's change that we are sharing (Colossians 4:2–6; 1 Peter 2:9-10).

Evangelism is the sharing of good news. News is propagated through words. Alvin Reid defined evangelism as "sharing the good news of Jesus Christ by word and life through the power of the Holy Spirit, so that unbelievers become followers of Jesus Christ in His church and in the culture."[75] In other words, redeemed-foreigners are called to share the good news of Jesus Christ in order that others may also become redeemed-foreigners who are filled with the Holy spirit, in turn being empowered to impact others in this world. Evangelism is not a task reserved for the few. It is a task for the whole church.

Preaching

It is no secret that the preaching of God's Word has declined in recent decades. Expository preaching has been replaced by self-help talks that promote shallow Christianity. Jim Shaddix, writing about Martyn-Loyd Jones' concerns back in nineteenth-century America, points out, "He was seeing the very beginning of a trend where entertainment, oratory, people-centered messages, and other pragmatic considerations were crowding out passionate biblical preaching."[76]

Unfortunately, the trend continued. Since then, Shaddix points out, "the most popular books on preaching tend to be those preoccupied with meeting people's "felt needs," being "relevant," being "practical," being "user-friendly," being "contemporary," or otherwise adapting the message to fit the hearers' preferences." The exaltation of Christ should be the focus of all preaching. This exaltation is accomplished when the text of the Bible is central in the sermon. I do recognize that there are preachers who are necessarily expositional in their approach who are used by God.

God's people need to be fed God's Word. Scripture was given to us in part of the nourishment of our souls. So, when our souls are malnourished through man-centered moralistic preaching the church suffers. I believe expository preaching provides a steady diet for the spiritual nourishment of God's Word to God's people. I define expository preaching as the proclamation of God's Word from a main pericope of Scripture from which the preacher derives the main content for his sermon. Such preaching is rooted in explanation, illustration, and application, derived from the meaning of the text as intended by the original author under the guidance of the Holy Spirit, ultimately leading God's people to transformation.[77]

Different preachers use different methods for preaching. The problem arises when preaching turns into a self-help talk to make people "feel" better. First, when preaching is overtly pragmatic it tends to be anthropocentric and earthly focused. Further, preachers fall prey to moralizing the text. It encourages people to follow a list of dos and don'ts that is fueled by guilt and fear rather than the glory of God. Second, this type of preaching fails to empower believers to live gospel-centered lives that point others to Christ versus looking for "your best life now." The gospel message is more about God than it is people. Though Christ died for the ungodly and has redeemed foreigners bound for hell, his ultimate goal was his own glorification, not our earthly betterment.

Albert Mohler highlights six main reasons why contemporary preaching suffers nowadays. First, contemporary preaching suffers from a loss of confidence in the power of the word. Second, it suffers from an infatuation with technology. Third, it suffers from embarrassment before the biblical text. Fourth, it suffers from an emptying of biblical content. Fifth, it suffers from a focus on felt needs. Sixth, it suffers from an absence of the gospel. [78] Most of Mohler's reasons highlight the lack of focus on Scripture. When we move away from the preaching of God's word to certain models of pulpit entertainment we are simply itching people's ears.

Ashford writes, "Although our evangelical churches have declared their belief that the Scriptures are *ipsissima verba Dei*, the very words of God, our declaration is not always consistent with our actions."[79] One of the reasons why the centrality of God's word matters in the local church is that right preaching, leads to right action. A fancy way to say it is, right orthodoxy (correct belief) leads to right orthopraxy (correct action). The expository preaching of God's Word provides the steady diet redeemed-foreigners need to be nourished while on their earthly pilgrimage.

Worship

I believe God-centered, Christ-exalting, Holy Spirit filled worship is also a mark of a healthy local church. Worship points us toward our heavenly destination. As I noted earlier from Gonzalez, "Worship is also an act of rehearsal."[80] One day all redeemed-foreigners will worship the Lord as heavenly citizens in the heavenly city of Jerusalem.

It is also through our worship that the world is able to identify to whom our allegiance belongs. As Reid puts it, "Witness and worship go together! Likewise, it matters that no corner of creation be exempt from exposure to the glory of God. Thus, the mission of God, the very thing God created Adam and Eve for: worshipping God and spreading that worship to the uttermost reaches of creation."[81] Part of letting our light shine so that God is glorified (Matthew 5:16) is related to worship. But what is worship?

In contemporary times worship is generally equated with music. This idea stems from the various examples in Scripture where God's people praise him through songs. One of the earliest examples of worship singing in Scripture is found in Exodus 15, just after the Israelites crossed the Jordan. In the Old Testament the book of Psalms highlights the importance of worshipful music. For instance, "Give thanks to the Lord with the lyre; make melody to him with the harp of ten strings!" (Psalm 33:2); "Oh sing to the Lord a new song, ... Make a joyful noise to the Lord, all the earth, break forth into joyous song and sing praises!" (Psalm 98:1,4). Furthermore, throughout church history many musicians have taken biblical passages and turned them into song.

A vibrant church will seek to honor God through the use of music. However, music is not the end goal of God-centered adoration; worship is. When music is equated with worship, all other forms of worship are diminished. The problem with this narrow view of worship is that it robs the local church of appreciating other types of worship activities. Worship in the local church is expressed in a variety of ways. It is expressed through service as ushers and greeters welcome others into the gathering of saints. Worship happens when God's people partake of the Lord's Supper, celebrate baptisms, child dedications, engage in local mission outreach, serve in kids and youth ministries, and when others disciple, teach, and lead other church members.

Worship services should allow room for different expressions of praise and adoration. All elements of a worship service work in harmony in order for worship to take place. Giving and tithing are an expression of worship. When giving of our treasures we remind ourselves of the fact that Christ gave himself for us. Reciting God's word out loud as a congregation is an expression of worship. When a congregation reads God's Word out loud it unites in its common understanding of the centrality of Scripture. Dancing is also an expression of worship. In the Old Testament people like king David, and others, expressed their worship through dancing. Finally, partaking of the sacraments of baptism and the Lord's Supper should also be a regular expression of worship in local congregations.

Finally, it is important to remember that worship, whether it be through music, serving, giving, or otherwise, should lead God's people to direct their thoughts and hearts toward heaven. If you're wondering what we will be doing for all eternity, just take a quick guess … worship! When God created Adam and Eve he put him and her into the garden of Eden "to serve it and to keep it" (Genesis 2:15). This language is referenced in Ezekiel in relation to the temple of God. In fact, Ezekiel refers to the temple as Eden, the "Garden of God" (Ezekiel 28:13).

Indeed, our worship is but a rehearsal of a greater future reality. One day redeemed-foreigners will exalt Christ as eternal heavenly citizens on God's holy mountain (Ezekiel 28:14). In the end, which will be the beginning of our eternal dwelling in the presence of God, on that holy mountain we will worship the Lord forever together. G. K. Beale points out, "The prophet

Ezekiel portrays Eden on a mountain (Ezekiel 28:14, 16). Israel's temple was on Mount Zion (e.g., Exodus 15:17), and the end-time temple was to be located on a mountain (Ezekiel 40:2; 43:12; Revelation 21:10)."[82] Until then, I hope you and I never feel at home in this world:

> This world is not my home, I'm just a passing through
> My treasures are laid up somewhere beyond the blue;
> The angels beckon me from heaven's open door,
> *And I can't feel at home in this world anymore.*
>
> O Lord, you know I have no friend like you,
> If heaven's not my home, then Lord what will I do?
> The angels beckon me from heaven's open door,
> *And I can't feel at home in this world anymore.*
>
> They're all expecting me, and that's one thing I know,
> My Savior pardoned me and now I onward go;
> I know He'll take me thro' tho' I am weak and poor,
> *And I can't feel at home in this world anymore.*
>
> I have a loving Savior up in glory-land,
> I don't expect to stop until I with Him stand,
> He's waiting now for me in heaven's open door.
> *And I can't feel at home in this world anymore.*
>
> Just up in glory-land we'll live eternally,
> The saints on every hand are shouting victory,
> Their songs of sweetest praise drift back from heaven's shore,
> *And I can't feel at home in this world anymore.*

> —— "This World is Not My Home" by
> Albert E. Brumley

CONCLUSION

Guess what? God does not want you to be a non-redeemed foreigner, condemned to eternal exile. He created us to live in fellowship and harmony with him. Creation's original design was perfect. But sin exiled us from God's presence after the Fall. The effects of our foreignness can be felt today. Every day we deal with the consequences of our sin. Sin's effects on us have eternal consequences. We know this world is broken and it is not our home. We are foreigners on earth. But this world is not our final destination. Neither is it our home.

Eden was humanity's first home. Before the Fall humanity was able to enjoy the bliss of living in a place without evil. But sin earned us exile. After the garden, humanity become increasingly corrupted by sin. Like a virus, sin spread to all mankind. But sin is more than a virus, it is part of our spiritual DNA. Therefore, all humans are born sinful. We are born enemies of God. Because we have been alienated from God, we are foreigners.

Without God we are non-redeemed foreigners. This means our final destination is eternal exile away from fellowship with God. But there is an alternative. God chose for himself a people from whom redemption would come. Indeed, redemption came. It came in the form of the perfect sinless Son of God,

Jesus Christ, the ultimate foreigner. The difference between Christ and us is that he was born of the Holy Spirit. He was born without sin. Though he experienced all the temptations we as earthly foreigners experience daily, he did not sin.

The importance of Christ's journey from heaven to earth cannot be overstated. He entered earth's realm as a foreigner to redeem foreigners. He came to turn all who come to him by faith into redeemed-foreigners. He came to pave the way, through his death on the cross, for our heavenly citizenship. The Bible shows us that after the garden, God chose a mountain to draw all peoples to praise him. That mountain is Mount Zion. There all the nations of the earth will bow down before Christ.

Mount Zion also represents a city. And guess who lives in cities? Citizens! God will one day we will enjoy our heavenly citizenship. Ephesians 2:6 tells us that we are already "seated in heavenly places." In other words, we are already citizens of the kingdom, but we live with the tension of the "already, not yet" or God's kingdom. Until then, those who believe in Christ by faith are redeemed-foreigners in the world on mission for God awaiting the city God promised. As heavenly-citizens we will enjoy eternal joy in the presence of God. There will be no more suffering, no more pain, no more sorrow for those who receive heavenly citizenship.

In the meantime, as a redeemed-foreigner, do not forget your identity, who you are in Christ. Make sure your earthly journey counts. Live a holy God as a representative of God's kingdom. Leave a legacy that impacts the world starting with your family, through how you live in society, and by honoring God in your faith community. Heed the words of the apostle Paul and "seek the things that are above, where Christ is, seated at the hand of God. Set your mind on things above, not things on earth" (Colossians 3:1–2).

As heavenly citizens redeemed foreigners will have full rights as children of God. And Guess What? You're invited to become one! All you have to do is repent, believe, and obey. Redeemed-foreigners will enjoy sharing in the inheritance God promises to all who believe and submit to him. I pray that you will, and that one day we will both worship the Lord in his presence as heavenly citizens.

[1] C. S. Lewis, Mere Christianity (New York, NY: Mcmillan, 1952), 135.

[2] https://www.lexico.com/en/definition/permanent

[3] https://en.oxforddictionaries.com/definition/immigration

[4] W. E. Vine, *Vine's Complete Expository Dictionary of Old and New Testament Words: With Topical Index* (Nashville, TN: T. Nelson, 1996), 50. "The wholly gracious and effective character of God's "covenant" is confirmed in the Septuagint by the choice of *diatheke* to translate *berith*. A *diatheke* is a will that distributes one's property after death according to the owner's wishes. It is completely unilateral. In the New Testament, *diatheke* occurs 33 times and is translated in the KJV 20 times as "covenant" and 13 times as "testament." In the RSV and the NASB, only "covenant" is used.

[5] https://www.blueletterbible.org/Comm/stewart_don/faq/bible-special/question4-why-old-and-new-testament.cfm.

[6] Kevin DeYoung and Greg Gilbert, *What is the Mission of the Church?* (Wheaton: Crossway, 2011), 70. The same idea is shared by many scholars. Alvin Reid. *Evangelism Handbook* (Nashville, TN: B & H Publishing Group, 2014), 51, writes, "We must increasingly proclaim the good news in the larger sense of the story of redemption–creation, fall, redemption, consummation." (Handbook on Evangelism, 51). Also see,

[7] Here I write that Adam "heard" the Lord walking in the garden, because that is what the original text says, "and they heard the voice of the Lord God walking in the garden."

[8] Gordon John Wenham, David Allen Hubbard, Glenn W. Barker. *Genesis 1–15*. Volume 1. Word Biblical Commentary. Grand Rapids, MI: Zondervan Academics, 1995.

[9] The amount of time Adam and Eve lived in the Garden of Eden is unknown. However, prior to the Fall, that was all that they had known.

[10] Keller, Timothy. *Center Church: Doing Balanced, Gospel-Centered Ministry in Your City* (Grand Rapids: Zondervan, 2012).

[11] Dempster, Stephen G. *Dominion and Dynasty: A Biblical Theology of the Hebrew Bible*. Downers Grove, IL: InterVarsity Press, 2006), 74.

[12] *Sarah* – "Sarah lived 127 years; these were the years of the life of Sarah. And Sarah died at Kiriath-arba (that is, Hebron) in the land of Canaan, and Abraham went in to mourn for Sarah and to weep for her" (Genesis 23:1). *Abraham* - "These are the days of the years of Abraham's life, 175 years. Abraham breathed his last and died in a good old age, an old man and full of years, and was gathered to his people" (Genesis 25:7-8).

[13] Wellum and Parker. *Progressive Covenantalism: Charting a Course Between Dispensational and Covenantal Theologies* (Nashville: B&H, 2016), 14.

[14] See, Word Biblical Commentary.

[15] "Now Moses was keeping the flock of his father-in-law, Jethro, the priest of Midian, and he led his flock to the west side of the wilderness and came to Horeb, the mountain of God" (Exodus 3:1).

[16] C.f.: https://www.bls.gov/spotlight/2013/foreign-born/

[17] C.f. https://legaldictionary.net/inalienable-rights/

[18] S. Barabas, "Foreigner," *The Zondervan Pictorial Encyclopedia of the Bible*, ed. Merrill C. Tenney (Grand Rapids: Zondervan Pub. House, 1975), 590.

[19] S. Barabas, "Foreigner," *The Zondervan Pictorial Encyclopedia of the Bible*, 590.

[20] James M. Hamilton (2010). *God's Glory in Salvation Through Judgment: A Biblical Theology* (Wheaton, IL: Crossway, 2010), 508.

[21] Lewis, C. S. (2014). *Weight of Glory*, (New York, NY: HarperCollins, 2014), 25–26.

[22] Hamilton, 234-235.

[23] Akin, Jonathan. Preaching Christ from Proverbs (p. 22).

[24] Graeme Goldsworthy. Christ-Centered Biblical Theology: Hermeneutical Foundations and Principles (Downers Grove, IL: IVP Academic), Kindle location1402-1404.

[25] Hamilton, 94). Crossway.

[26] Jonathan Akin. *Preaching Christ from Proverbs* (United States: Crossway, 2001), 36–37, points out, "He returned to Egypt by marrying Pharaoh's daughter (1 Kings 3:1), he accumulated wives (1 Kings 11:1-3), and he accumulated money (1 Kings 10:14-29)—actions which lead to the ruin of his dynasty (Deut 17:16-17). Akin, Jonathan. Preaching Christ from Proverbs.

[27] Akin, 22.

[28]   https://www.blueletterbible.org/lang/lexicon/lexicon.cfm?Strongs=H5030&t=KJV

[29] Hamilton, 256.

[30] DeYoung and Gilbert, 81.

[31] Wellum and Parker. *Progressive Covenantalism: Charting a Course Between Dispensational and Covenantal Theologies* (Nashville: B&H, 2016), 25.

[32] Roy Ciampa. "Toward the Effective Preaching of New Testament Texts that Cite the Old Testament," in *Preaching the Old Testament*. Edited by Scott M. Gibson (Grand Rapids, MI: Baker Publishing Group, 2006), 166.

[33] Hamilton, 51.

[34] Hamilton, pp. 51-52.

[35] Robert Coleman, "Preaching the Old Testament Evangelistically," in *Preaching the Old Testament*. Edited by Scott M. Gibson (Grand Rapids, Baker Publishing Group), 190.

[36] John Piper. *Let the Nations Be Glad!* (Grand Rapids, MI: Baker Publishing Group, 2010), Kindle Location 4200.

[37] C. S. Lewis, *Weight of Glory*, 26.

[38] Spurgeon, C. H. *Gleanings Among the Sheaves* (Harrisburg, PA: Christian Publications, 1975), 57.

[39] González, J. L. *For the Healing of the Nations: The Book of Revelation in an Age of Cultural Conflict*. (Maryknoll, N.Y.: Orbis Books, 1999), 109.

[40] Akin, p. 84.

[41] Philip O. Hopkins, "Mission and Unreached People Groups," in Theology and Practice of Missions. Edited by Bruce Riley Ashford. (Nashville: B&H, 2011), 173.

[42] Bruce R. Ashford, "A Theologically Driven Missiology," in Theology and Practice of Missions. Edited by Bruce Riley Ashford. (Nashville: B&H, 2011), 16.

[43] Hamilton, 787.

[44] Philip O. Hopkins, "Mission and Unreached People Groups," 173.

[45] Hamilton, 53.

[46] David Jones, *Men, Women, and the Meaning of Marriage* (Self-published, Copyright 2012) Kindle location 242.

[47] John MacArthur. *The MacArthur Study Bible New American Standard Bible* (Nashville, TN: Nelson Bibles, 2014), 21.

[48] https://www.marriage.com/advice/love/10-tips-to-bring-more-love-and-respect-into-your-marriage/

[49] More can be said here about morality. I work from the premise that morality is divinely originated. It has its basis in the person of God. He is both a giver and originator of morality. Without God-based morality, our morals are shaped by relativism. It comes down to the issue of moral authority. Parents are not the arbiters of morality; they are simply tasked by God (my personal view) to raise their children to follow his divinely given principles.

[50] You can also teach your children from the Heidelberg Catechism, *Cornerstones Parent Guide* by Brian Dembowczyk, or *A New Baptist Catechism: Important Questions and Answers to Instruct Children About God and the Gospel* by Dwayne Milioni.

[51] Alvin Reid. *Life Is a Mission Trip—TAKE IT! A Practical Guide to Shar-*

ing Jesus (Be Inspired Books, 2021), 60.

[52] https://www.biblestudytools.com/classics/barnes-scenes-in-life/the-voyage-to-rome/

[53] Edward L. Smither. Mission in the Early Church: Themes and Reflections (Eugene, OR: Cascade Books, 2014), 154.

[54] Sam Chan, How to Talk About Jesus Without Being That Guy: Personal Evangelism in a Skeptical World (Grand Rapids, MI: Zondervan Reflective, 2020), 47.

[55] Schmidt, How Christianity Changed the World, 8.

[56] DeYoung and Gilbert, 249.

[57] https://www.christianheadlines.com/contributors/milton-quintanilla/john-piper-warns-christians-not-to-place-patriotism-over-christ-the-church.html

[58] DeYoung and Gilbert, 130.

[59] https://www.merriam-webster.com/dictionary/influencer

[60] https://bamglobal.org/about/

[61] https://bamglobal.org/report-biblical/

[62] David Platt, Radical: Taking Back your Faith from the American Dream (Colorado Springs: Multnomah, 2010), 156.

[63] STRONGS NT 4964.

[64] Keith Whitfield "The Triune God: The God of Mission," in *A Theology and Practice of Mission: God, the Church, and the Nations*, ed. Bruce Riley Ashford (Nashville, TN: B & H Publishing Group, 2011), 22.

[65] Piper, Let the Nations Be Glad, Kindle location 547.

[66] Coleman, "The Agents of Mission: Humanity," 43.

[67] Concerning hell, DeYoung and Gilbert write, "The doctrine of hell is like that for the church. Divine wrath may not be the decorative masthead or the flag we raise up every flagpole. The doctrine may be underneath other doctrines. It may not always be seen. But its absence will always be felt", DeYoung and Gilbert, *What is the Mission of the Church?*, 245.

[68] Köstenberger and O'Brien, *Salvation to the Ends of the Earth*, 19.

[69] Jürgen Moltmann, *The Church in the Power of the Spirit* (New York, NY: Harper & Row, 1977), 10.

[70] Michael Goheen, *A Light to the Nations* (Grand Rapids, MI: Baker Academic, 2011), 4.

[71] Goheen, *A Light to the Nations*, 4.

[72] https://joshuaproject.net.

[73] https://www.9marks.org/about/the-nine-marks/

[74] Harvey M. Conn, "Culture," in *Evangelical Dictionary of World Mission*, ed. A. Scott Moreau (Grand Rapids, MI: Baker Book House Co., 2000), np.

[75] Reid, Evangelism Handbook, 31.

[76] James Shaddix. *The Passion-Driven Sermon: Changing the Way Pastors Preach and Congregations Listen* (Nashville, TN: B&H Publishing Group, 2003), Kindle location 69.

[77] See, https://thepreachersdevoblog.com/what-is-expository-preaching/.

[78] Albert Mohler, R. He is Not Silent (Chicago, IL: Moody Publishers, 2008), 16.

[79] Bruce Riley Ashford. *Theology & Practice of Mission* (Nashville: B&H, 2011), 294.

[80] See quote on page 86.

[81] Evangelism Handbook, Reid, 51.

[82] G. K. Beale, *The Temple and the Church's Mission: A biblical theology of the dwelling place of God* (Downers Grove, IL: InterVarsity Press, 2004), 73.

ABOUT THE AUTHOR

Daniel C. Messina

Daniel Messina was born and raised in Brazil. His wife Ashli and three sons (Gabriel, Joshua, and Joel) are one of his greatest joys in life. He holds a Bachelor's degree in Christian Studies with an Emphasis in Theology and a Minor in Biblical Hebrew. He earned his Master of Arts in old Testament studies from Southeastern Baptist Theological Seminary. Daniel has worked in full time ministry for 15 years in multiple capacities. He enjoys writing blogs for the preachersdevoblog.com and is also the Podcast host for The Preacher's Devotional Podcast, currently on iTunes and Spotify.